Ojibwe Hunter

Ojibwe-giiyosewinini

(Ojib-way-ge-key-o-say-wi-ni-ni)

Blue Hand Books, Greenfield, MA

Ojibwe Hunter:
True Hunting, Fishing and Trapping Stories on Vince Shute's Property before his Black Bear Sanctuary Opened
(1971-1988)

By James Chavers Jr.
(Bois Fort Band of Ojibwe)

Jim at the billboard to the Vince Shute Black Bear Sanctuary (Family Photo)

Native American/Hunting Stories

© 2013 James Chavers Jr.
James Chavers Jr. is a member of the Bois Forte- Nett Lake Band of Ojibwe in
Minnesota

Ojibwe Hunter: True Hunting, Fishing and Trapping Stories on Vince Shute's
Property before his Black Bear Sanctuary Opened (2013) by James Chavers Jr.

ISBN: 978-1482004977

ISBN-10: 1482004976

Chavers, James [1956-]

Charles Grolla wrote Traditional Ojibwe Hunting, Animal Chapters and Ojibwe
glossary as noted.

Publisher: BLUE HAND BOOKS
442 Main Street, # 1061
Greenfield, MA 01301
www.bluehandbooks.org

Cover design: Trace DeMeyer
Photos by James Chavers, Charles Grolla and family

First Edition 2013

Dedicated to Vince Shute

Vince Shute and one of his Black Bears (Chavers Photo)

FROM THE AUTHOR

James Chavers Jr.

Ah-neen! Hello. *Ojibwe Hunter* is a collection of my true wildlife hunting, fishing and trapping stories that took place on Vince Shute's property before his Black Bear Sanctuary opened near my reservation in Nett Lake, Minnesota.

I am half Chippewa (Bois Forte) and half Irish. I was born June 17, 1956, in Cook, Minnesota. My mom Josephine married three times and raised 14 kids; today five of us are still here. My tribe has over 3,000 members and I am enrolled. My dad James Chavers Sr. left when I was six; I have more siblings in his family, too.

I hunted ducks and geese on Nett Lake all my life. I started when I was eight years old. Since 1966, I worked as a guide for non-Indian duck and geese hunters every autumn on Nett Lake, home of the world's biggest and best wild rice crop in Minnesota. Every fall, September to October, I riced for a living, bringing in 300-600 pounds of wild rice a day. I hand-parched my wild rice and sold it for $10 per pound. With my good earnings I was able to buy my hunting guns and nice cars.

I have hundreds of stories; many took place after I met Vince Shute in 1968 when I was 12 years old. My oldest brother Dale Leecy had told me a lot about Vince and his dock on Lost River. I put five ducks in my backpack and walked to Vince's trailer house and knocked on his door. He lived alone and was about 1 1/2 miles off the Nett Lake reservation boundaries. Vince answered his door and asked my name. I told him I was Jim Chavers Jr. and Dale was my oldest brother.

"What brings you down here?" he asked.

"I was jump-shooting mallard ducks down on Lost River," I said, and then I pulled those ducks out and gave Vince his dinner.

He thanked me big time. I told him I had a long paddle home so he shook my hand and said, "Jim Chavers, anytime you want something, don't be afraid to ask."

We became the best of friends. Vince lived about four miles from my mother Josephine's house. Because I brought him duck and deer meat, Vince only allowed **me** to trap and hunt on his property.

Over the years, I shot 100+ deer on top of this big rock a half a mile away from Vince Shute's trailer house. I visited Vince at least three times a month when I hunted deer, too. I took him out hunting ducks a few times. I also shot Bull Moose and timber wolves and more deer down towards Lost River on a big hilly rocky ravine.

There is a trail that goes to Lost River from Vince's trailer house. He and I both called it the Black Bear Trail. In the 1970s and 80s there was a lot of black bears hanging around Vince's trailer house. I told Vince he should put an ad in the newspaper about all the black bears coming around his place. I said he should let people come and pay him to take pictures. He said he'd think about it.

Vince fed the bears peanuts and other nuts. He even talked to the bears. He would mumble something in their ears and they listened. There was even an albino black bear hanging around in 1973-1977. The bears would come and go as they pleased.

Over the years, I hunted moose, timber wolves, lynx, bobcats, wolverine, and even shot a few wild dogs. I trapped fisher, rabbit, beaver, otter, muskrat, mink, weasel, raccoon and fox every winter. I use my high-powered rifles with scopes, automatic and pump shotguns, and the single shot 36 inch Long Tom for Bull Moose and deer. I used shotguns for ducks and geese.

My family loves to eat moose, deer meat, roast duck and geese with wild rice stuffing, and partridge and pheasant. I also fish so we ate plenty of walleye, musky, croppies, bass, blue gills, suckers, bullheads, cat fish and sturgeon.

I talked with Vince Shute on a few occasions about starting a black bear sanctuary. I knew a lot of people would love to see his bears. Vince died in 2000 and donated his land to Orr, Minnesota, 15 miles away from his home. He didn't have any family. The town built a big black bear sanctuary where his trailer house sat on his property in 2004.

Tourists from all over the world visit now. One photographer took a photo of an albino black bear and black bear sniffing each other. The gift shop sells thousands of that one photograph.

In all those years, Vince had me shoot only two aggressive male black bears. Back then 40-50 bear would hang around all summer. Some might migrate up to Ely, Minnesota, about 80 miles away but many hibernated down in the hilly rocky ravines country on Lost River near his place.

When I was 16 in 1973, a drunk driver hit me on my motorcycle. I broke 12 bones and was in a coma for three days and had blood clots in my brain. When I was 28, I got into a head-on car accident in Minneapolis and spent 18 months in a full-body cast. Despite short term memory loss from a stroke on June 3, 1999 which left me paralyzed on my right side, I can still remember all my hunting stories.

Vince Shute let me hunt and trap on his property for over 30 years. Vince truly was my best friend so I dedicate this book to him and his memory.

TRADITIONAL OJIBWE HUNTING

By Charles Grolla

To the Ojibwe hunter, hunting is a spiritual event that is taken very serious. It is not a sport like most hunters think and classify the activity of hunting.

Before colonization, the Ojibwe were primarily a fishing people using all resources available to them to survive and did so by fishing, hunting, trapping, gathering wild rice, gathering berries, gardening and foraging for edible plants. While using all resources around them, they did not waste anything and took only what was needed; life depended on those resources.

Ojibwe believe that everything has a soul, purpose, and everything exists in balance with one another. With that being said, it is common knowledge to all Native Americans that we live in a spiritual world and all things and beings are connected to each other and are to be respected. Anything that is taken from nature, be it a flower picked from the forest and taken home, to a deer killed and fed to the family, an offering of tobacco was given to its spirit, thus keeping the balance. If we take something we need to give back and be respectful because everything has a spirit.

The Ojibwe tradition and belief with hunting is that animals give themselves to the hunter by taking pity on the hunter and that those animals are providing food for them and their family to live. In turn these animals are respected with a tobacco offering (*asema*) at the site of the kill and certain traditional procedures are done depending on the kind of animal.

When a person, male or female makes their first kill on any animal, bird or fish, a ceremony is done and the animal, fish or bird is given away to community members as a sign of respect to the animal, fish or bird.

These ceremonies continue today and in the Ojibwe language, this first kill ceremony is called Oshkinitaagewin (o-shke-ni-taw-gay-win). Although women do hunt, mainly males while growing up were groomed to hunt; the Oshkinitaagewin ceremony is for either male or female. This was done for each first kill of a species: First rabbit, first fish, first deer, etc.

Every Ojibwe person has a clan and it is one of the twenty-plus clans that exist among the Ojibwe Nation. Clan members view each other as family members, kind of like how we use last names nowadays. There are strict rules of no marriage between clan members and one should not eat or hunt his own clan animal, bird or fish. The Ojibwe word for Clan is *Doodem*. The clan system for the Ojibwe is patrilineal meaning the a person's clan is passed down by his father, in some cases with a non-native father or father of a different tribe, the person is adopted by either the *Migizi* (bald eagle) or *Waabizheshii* (Pine marten) clan depending on the area one lives. For additional information, a respected elder of the one's community or area they are from can be sought and with a small gift of tobacco can be asked the questions of what tradition they use and go by. This is another reason that animals are hunted with care and respect because it could be someone's clan. Clan is also called *totem* in the English language.

Charles Grolla is Jim Chaver's nephew.

HUNTING DUCKS AND WHITE-TAILED DEER

October 1971 (Wiggie and me)

Chapter One

I asked my mother, Josephine Chavers, if she could drop me and my dog Wiggie off out at the reservation line early the next morning. We were going to hunt ducks and deer.

She said, "Good, I will sharpen up the knives." Mother knew I was a good hunter, even then at age 15. I'd started hunting at a very young age and I always bought a hunting license for when I hunted off my rez and on Vince Shute's land.

Wiggie was the best little hunting dog ever! Wiggie was a brown and white mutt I'd raised from a pup. He only weighed 35 pounds and was about 14 inches tall. (His brother Bully was 16 inches tall and 45 pounds and black and white.) Wiggie would sniff the ground, making loud sniffing noises, and tree partridges or spruce hens. He was also a very smart deer hunter. If I crippled a deer and it ran away over two or three miles, Wiggie would find it and start barking. The deer would be dead from the loss of blood, or too weak from the loss of blood to run anymore. Then I would shoot it dead. Wiggie also retrieved ducks for me, even if there was thin, cold ice on the lakes.

The Nett Lake Indian Reservation line is right across the road north of Vince Shute's property. About one-half mile down the reservation line on the south side of the road, about a quarter-mile back, there is a big duck slough hole. This country, including Vince's property, is abundant with wildlife, especially white-tailed deer. About three-quarters of a mile past the first big duck slough hole, there is a bigger duck slough hole. I have shot hundreds of mallards and different kinds of ducks out of both slough holes. I also shot a lot of huge bucks, a few massive swamp bucks; I trapped a lot of fur animals in this area and also on Vince Shute's property.

I fed Wiggie a good meal that Friday night. While petting him I said, "Wiggie, let's go hunting ducks and deer early tomorrow morning." He got all excited while eating; he began whining and wagging his tail.

Mother and I watched TV that Friday night. The ten o'clock news predicted light rain and dark, low clouds for the northern part of Minnesota. My mother said, "Good weather for hunting ducks and deer." I told Mother that I would use my Remington three-inch Magnum single-shot with a 36-inch barrel Long-Tom. I had two boxes of three-inch Magnum two-shot B. B. loads shells, one box of three-inch Magnum hollow-point slugs, and one box of three-inch Magnum buckshot. I put the four boxes of shells in my backpack along with my rain jacket in case it started to rain. The rut mating season for deer and moose was on.

At about 10:30 p.m. Friday night I called my little dog, Wiggie, to come inside the house; he always slept by my bed in my bedroom at night. That is his reward for all the ducks he has retrieved for me, and the crippled deer he has tracked down for me in the past four years. After I had set my alarm clock for 5 a.m., I talked to and petted Wiggie, rubbing his ears. Then I went to bed.

Chapter Two

Waking to the sound of my alarm clock ringing, I shut it off and got up for the day. Like every other morning, Wiggie was whining, jumping around and scratching the bedroom door. He was anxious to get outside to relieve himself and sniff around his territory. After I was dressed, and when Wiggie and I were leaving the bedroom, I could smell fried deer meat and fresh coffee. Once Wiggie was outside, I said good morning to my mother. She answered, "Good morning. For breakfast I cooked you deer meat, eggs, and pancakes with coffee." I thanked her, and then she said, "You better give Wiggie a plate of the food." I told her I would as soon as he was done checking outside. I dished up Wiggie a double portion of the tasty food and went outside to feed him.

After coming back inside and taking care of a few errands, I then went into the kitchen and ate my delicious breakfast. Mother told me that she made me four deer-meat sandwiches and a thermos of coffee, putting them in my backpack. Around 5:50 a.m. I told Mother I would warm up her old truck. When I went outside Wiggie was there, jumping around, all excited because he knew we were going hunting. As soon as I started Mother's truck, Wiggie jumped in the back and started whining. I said to Wiggie, "It's okay, I'm not leaving you." Rubbing his ears and side, I told Wiggie to stay in the back of the pickup.

Once I was back in the house, Mother said, "Wiggie sure is excited to go hunting."

I said, "So am I!" Mother laughed, putting on her rain jacket.

The sky was covered with low, dark clouds, but it was only sprinkling out.

After grabbing my backpack, Wiggie and I were ready to go hunting. Mother drove us three miles out to the reservation line. When she let us off, she wished us good luck with our hunt. I told her not to worry about picking us up; Wiggie and I would catch a ride home. She said, "Okay," turned the pickup around, and headed back to Nett Lake.

It was just getting light outside. Wiggie was already sniffing around as we headed down the Reservation Line Road. Wiggie was a smart deer hunter, sitting quietly next to me as we waited for deer to walk down the deer trail coming toward us. He would always let me know when deer were coming. He would sniff the air, his ears moving back and forth. Then he would look at me and then look the way that the deer were coming from. Thanks to Wiggie, I had shot many deer like that.

It was starting to sprinkle rain a little harder, so I took my rain jacket out of my backpack and put it on. We arrived at the small, old trail that led to the first duck slough hole. Wiggie's ears were going back and forth. We could hear the mallards quacking by the hundreds, even though it was sprinkling out. Those mallards were about a quarter-mile away. Then I spotted a big flock of mallards flying toward the duck slough hole just above the tree level, about 100 yards in front of us. Looking up, Wiggie saw them too, so we walked to the duck slough hole. There were all kinds of ducks quacking, mostly mallards.

When we were about 100 yards away from them, I could see black mallards and green-headed mallards sitting on old dead logs in the water. There also were local bluebills, teals, redheads, canvasbacks, and pintail ducks. I took the buckshot out of my Long-Tom and replaced it with a three-inch Magnum two-shot B. B. load. I had butterflies in my stomach. Wiggie was anxious to go retrieve some ducks. I couldn't make my mind up which ducks to dry-gulch first, the ones swimming in the water that were bunched up or the black mallards lined up on the log.

Ducks and geese are not afraid of dogs, but they will fly away if a dog gets too close to them in the water. I lined up the black mallards on the log and shot. The whole duck slough hole erupted in ducks taking flight. I quickly ejected the spent shell, loaded my Long-Tom again and shot another black mallard out of the air. Wiggie was already swimming after a dead mallard that I had shot off of the log. I shot three black mallards dead as I lined them up. By then the rest of the ducks had flown out of shotgun range. Well, at least I shot four black mallards before they all flew out of range. There must have been around 1,000 ducks that took flight.

Wiggie was a smart little dog! He brought one black mallard back and dropped him by my feet. As I walked up to the edge of the duck slough hole, he went jumping and splashing into the water and retrieved another black mallard. I had to send him after the third and fourth black mallards. I put the four dead black mallards in my backpack.

Wiggie was sniffing around in the tall weeds next to the shoreline, and then he started whining and running around. From past experience, I knew Wiggie had the scent of something. I walked over to the tall weeds, pushed the weeds apart with the barrel of my Long-Tom, and in the mud I saw giant Bull Moose tracks. The tracks went out into the duck slough hole. I could tell that the tracks were about two days old. A huge bull moose was in the area! He must have gone through and out the other side of the duck slough hole somewhere.

Chapter Three

I petted and rubbed Wiggie's ears and said, "Wiggie, as you know, there is a huge bull moose in the area; if we see him, I will gun him down. But for now, we have another duck slough hole to hunt. Let's get going." Wiggie began whining and sniffing the ground, then headed toward the road.

We got about 300 yards or so away from the duck slough hole when Wiggie treed a partridge. The partridge was teasing Wiggie, looking down at him, making all kinds of chirping noises. So I took my backpack off and grabbed my shotgun. That partridge wasn't going to tease Wiggie anymore, I shot the partridge dead! Wiggie jumped on it and shook it around a few times to make sure that it was dead, and then brought the dead partridge over to me, dropping it at my feet. I praised Wiggie, rubbing his head and ears. Putting the partridge in my backpack with the ducks, Wiggie and I headed toward the road.

When we got to the road, my watch told me that the time was 7:20 a.m. I loaded my Long-Tom with three-inch Magnum buckshot in case we spooked a white-tailed buck. I would have a good chance of hitting him on the run with buckshot. It was about a one-mile walk to the bigger duck slough hole, so Wiggie and I slowly started walking in that direction. Sometimes when you walk, a deer standing will watch you walk right past them, and you won't see them. But with Wiggie with me, I do believe that we never walked past a deer.

Wiggie never went more than 50 yards ahead of me; he would run in every direction, sniffing the ground. We walked about 300 yards down the road and Wiggie treed two partridges. Slowly I took my backpack off. The partridges were looking down at Wiggie, making *weak, weak, weak* noises. Removing the buckshot from my shotgun, I replaced it with B. B. load and shot one partridge dead. The other bird flew off before I could get another shot off. Wiggie jumped on the dead partridge quickly, brought it over to me, and dropped it at my feet. I put the partridge in my backpack with the other kill, gave Wiggie his due praise by scratching behind his ears and petting him, then commending him with, "Good hunting, Wiggie." Showing his appreciation of the hunt, Wiggie was licking my fingers and wagging his tail.

After I reloaded my Long-Iom with three-inch Magnum buckshot, Wiggie and I again began walking toward the bigger duck slough hole. When we got to about a quarter-mile away from the slough, I could hear mallards quacking and geese honking. "Wiggie, do you hear those geese honking?" I asked. The twitching of his ears and the excited actions answered my question. We both were anxious to get closer, but we carefully walked forward toward the bigger slough hole, watching my steps so I didn't step on any dead branches, making noise that might alert the ducks and geese of our arrival. We crept within 50 yards of the birds, using the brush and tall weeds for cover. I held Wiggie and whispered to him quietly, "Keep quiet, Wiggie, we don't want to scare the geese and mallards away." Every now and then I could hear the mallards quacking and the geese honking. I could see that about 20 of them were snow geese, and there looked to be about 200 mallards in this bigger duck slough hole. I expected there to be a lot more ducks in this bigger slough hole.

Although he was excited to retrieve some ducks, Wiggie listened to me good when I told him to stay. I sneaked up to about 10 feet from the water, hiding well in the tall weeds. Wiggie nudged against me; I laughed to myself and whispered, "It's okay, Wiggie, I know you are excited too." The snow geese were sitting in the water about 50 yards out. Slowly I took off my backpack and loaded my Long-Tom with three-inch Magnum B. B. loads. I lined up two snow geese and shot; both stayed down, flapping their wings, going in circles on the water, then lay dead. The snow geese and the black- and green-headed mallards took flight. As I quickly reloaded my Long-Tom, Wiggie went splashing into the water after the two dead snow geese. I shot another snow goose before they got out of range.

Wiggie retrieved one of the snow geese and went splashing in the water after the second one. The snow geese were as big as Wiggie. I laughed to myself, thinking that it looked crazy to see Wiggie retrieve a goose that was as big as him. When Wiggie dropped the second snow goose at my feet, I had to point and send him after the third snow goose. He went splashing after it, which was about 100 yards out in the water. After Wiggie dropped the third snow goose at my feet, I petted him and rubbed his ears.

Then I heard mallards quacking. Coming at us above the trees were eight mallards. I shot a green-headed mallard that landed in the woods about 50 feet away from Wiggie and me. Wiggie pounced on the mallard in a split second and dropped the dead mallard by my feet. I said, "Good hunting, Wiggie." He jumped around, wagging his tail and sniffing around in the tall weeds. I put the three snow geese and mallard in my backpack, which was full to the limit with the four black mallards and two partridges. Then I said to Wiggie, "Let's go hunt white-tailed deer on Carden's Road."

Chapter Four

My watch gave the time as 10:45 a.m. Wiggie knew the way to Carden's Road, since we had hunted this area many times before. I loaded my Long-Tom with three-inch Magnum buckshot. Wiggie went on ahead of me. If he got 50 yards out front, Wiggie would stop sniffing around, look back at me, and then wait until I caught up with him. Then Wiggie would take off, sniffing the ground in every direction, repeating this performance over and over again until he treed a partridge or spruce hen.

South of the big duck slough hole there was an old logging road; follow that for about one-quarter of a mile and you would come to Carden's Road. Carden's Road was approximately 50 feet wide and about three-quarters of a mile long. After going about one-quarter of a mile down the road there was a big hill, around 300 yards up, then the road went straight for a little less than a half-mile, coming to a main highway. Several deer trails crossed Carden's Road. Wiggie and I took the old logging trail to Carden's Road and then began walking east.

I sat on top of an old log pile, poured a cup of coffee, and took out two deer-meat sandwiches. Wiggie was on the ground, sniffing the bottom of the old log pile. I called Wiggie over, so he ran up the old log pile, and I gave him a tasty deer-meat sandwich. It was turning out to be a nice fall day; the low dark clouds had disappeared, and the sun was shining. So I took off my rain jacket and put it in a side pocket of my backpack with my shotgun shells. Wiggie nudged me and started looking down Carden's Road. Approximately 200 yards down, there were two doe standing on the road. I had just looked that way about a minute ago and there hadn't been any deer standing there. Unloading the buckshot from my gun, I slowly reached in my backpack, taking out a box of three-inch Magnum hollow-point slugs, and reloaded my Long-Tom. It was the rut mating season, and from past experience watching the deer mating ritual, the does play hard to get and run when a buck comes. It's called courting.

I looked down at Wiggie and he was excitedly looking at the two does. We watched the two does for about five minutes, and then they both looked in the same direction toward the woods with their ears pointing upwards.

"Wiggie, I bet there is a buck coming," I whispered. Both does took off running in the woods down the deer trail. I told Wiggie to get ready. He looked at me and seemed to smile, then looked back down Carden's Road. I got butterflies in my stomach. Sure enough, after about three minutes time had passed since the does ran off, I could see a huge rack of horns come into sight, then the body of a large buck. He was standing on the edge of Carden's Road, sniffing the ground where the two does had been standing. I let him walk to the middle of Carden's Road, then I took aim with my Long-Tom open sights on his huge chest, and shot. I could hear a loud smack a split second later. The huge buck leaped high in the air and disappeared into the woods. Wiggie bounded down the old log pile and ran after the huge buck that I could hear making grunting noises. Loading my Long-Tom with buckshot, I grabbed my backpack, put it on, got off the log pile, and ran down to where the buck had been when I shot him. I could hear Wiggie barking about 200 yards back in the woods on the deer trail.

Near the edge of Carden's Road, on the deer trail, I spotted blood. Judging by the size of the drops of blood on the ground, I knew the buck couldn't run very far. Putting my backpack against a cedar tree, I began to run down the deer trail. About every 8 to 12 feet there were large blood splatters on the ground. First I saw Wiggie, and behind him, lying dead, was the large buck that had a rack of horns with six points on both sides. A 12-point buck! Petting Wiggie, I gave him praise for tracking down the buck. Wiggie was wagging his tail and licking my fingers in his show of appreciation.

I took out my knife and gutted out the big buck. I grabbed Wiggie and rubbed the buck's blood all over his face. Wiggie likes that and I had done that previously with many deer that I had shot and killed. I dragged the big buck by his horns out of the brush to the side of Carden's Road.

My watch gave the time to be 12:30 p.m., not bad for a half-day's hunting. After putting on my backpack, Wiggie and I headed for the main highway. When we got there we hitchhiked towards Nett Lake. It didn't take us long to catch a ride; the manager of the Nett Lake gas and grocery store picked Wiggie and me up. I put my backpack in the back seat and commanded Wiggie to jump in beside it. As we rode toward Nett Lake, the store manager asked me if I had had any luck in our hunt. I told him about our early success in shooting four black mallards, two partridges, three snow geese, and a big 12-point buck. The manager said, "Sounds like you did really good."

"Yes, if it wasn't for my good little hunting dog, Wiggie, I wouldn't have shot anything," I said while reaching back and rubbing little Wiggie's head and ears.

He let us off at my mother's house, and Wiggie and I went inside. I set my backpack on the kitchen table, and Wiggie ran up to my mother when she came into the room. She reached down to pet Wiggie, saying, "I was surprised to see you back so soon. That was a quick hunting trip." I told her about shooting the ducks, partridges, and geese, and then said, "We have to go and pick up that 12-point buck that I shot on Carden's Road!"

Mother got all excited and hurried off to get her truck keys. She drove Wiggie and me back out to Carden's Road. Mother helped me load the big buck into the pickup bed and we went home to process the deer I killed.

DUCK HUNTING WITH VINCE SHUTE

October 1972 (I am his guide)

Vince Shute and I planned to go hunt ducks and geese at 6:00 a.m. He drove his 4x4 Chevy truck to my mother's house at 5:15 a.m. My mother Josephine had coffee with us at 5:30 a.m. then Vince helped me load my canoe in the back of his truck. We took ten mallard decoys. Vince and I both said good-bye to my mother and she wished us good luck on our hunting trip.

Vince and I headed to Goofies Landing, about 1 ½ miles from my mother's house. We got there just as the sun was coming up. It was going to be a rainy, cloudy, dark day. We could hear the ducks quacking by the thousands. I told Vince, "It's going to be a great day for hunting ducks and geese. "

He agreed, "Sounds like it by all the ducks quacking."

Vince Shute and I unloaded my canoe and we put it in the water. Vince grabbed the 10 mallard decoys. I grabbed our other gear, paddles, lunch and 2 thermoses of hot coffee and put it all in the canoe. Vince grabbed his Remington automatic 12 gauge. I used my single-shot 36 inch barrel Winchester long tom. Vince brought five boxes of number 4 shot magnums. I brought three boxes of number four shot three inch magnums. I told Vince Shute to load his gun up right away.

There was a little island about 150 yards out called Goofies Island. We got in the canoe and Vince Shute paddled in the front, I paddled in the back. We headed towards Mallard Bay. Vince and I could see huge flocks of ducks flying in every direction.

I said, "Vince here comes five ducks to the left of us." I told him to shoot them as soon as they came into range. Vince shot two times and one duck folded up and hit the water with a splash. We picked the duck up; it was a black mallard.

Thousands of ducks took flight because of the loud shots. I told Vince Shute to be ready because ducks panic when they hear gun shots. We were in the thick wild rice, out of sight. It was getting better outside as time passed.

I told Vince, "Here comes some ducks on your left side." Seven northern blue bills came flying just above the thick wild rice. Vince Shute shot first, three quick shots, two northern blue bills hit the water. I aimed at the last northern blue bill; my gun snapped on an empty chamber, I forgot to put a shell in the chamber. Vince Shute burst out laughing really hard; then I did, too.

This time I put in a three-inch magnum in my long tom. Vince Shute looked at me kind of funny and said it's going to be an exciting day. I looked at Vince and smiled and said, "You got that right my friend!"

Vince Shute and I picked up the two northern blue bills that he shot and we continued down towards Mallard Bay.

Mallard Bay is about a two mile paddle, and then it swings right around for about one mile. Then it's about a two-mile paddle up to Gene Moler's Point. Goofies Landing is about one mile across from Gene Moler's Point. On the way to Mallard Bay, about half way down, there are three little grass islands. Vince Shute and I could see a lot of ducks flying past the third little grass island and swing down in Mallard Bay and land in the open water. I said, "Vince, let's go to that third little grass island and pass shoot ducks.

Vince Shute agreed, "Let's do it!"

As we got close to the first little grass island about 15 mallards jumped up close out of the thick wild rice. Vince quickly grabbed his cannon and shot two mallards out of the air. They hit the water in the thick wild rice with a splash, both deader than dead. We picked up the two mallards and paddled to the third little grass island and hid in the wild rice.

When we got to the third grass island, a flock of green winged teal flew right by Vince and me. We did not see them coming; they were flying so fast. I know ducks by their pattern of flight. Right after that, two canvas backs came flying to their death. Vince Shute folded them up with two shots. I was letting Vince Shute shoot most of the ducks today. That's the kind of guide I am.   A good guide will let his hunter shoot most of the ducks.

We waited about five minutes watching all kinds of different groups of ducks fly by. Vince Shute said, "Chavers, look down in Mallard Bay; a huge flock of Canadian geese took flight." They start honking like crazy. There must have been around 75 Canadian honkers.

"What a beautiful sight! I wish they flew right over us!" Vince said.

I said, "They are heading right over big island, going past Gene Moler's Point. They are going higher and higher." Sure enough they flew high towards Nett River and disappeared in the dark clouds. I paddled Vince Shute along the shoreline in the wild rice, jump shooting ducks. We headed back up towards Gene Moler's Landing across the lake from Goofies Landing. A big flock of northern blue bills were flying right at us. They were about 100 yards out. I told Vince to flock shoot them.

Vince shot three quick shots in the flock and two northern blue bills hit the water. One was dead the other one was crippled. He shot him again. We picked up the two northern blue bills and headed to Gene Moler's Point.

I decided to take Vince Shute to the narrows behind big island. The narrows are three grass islands in a row. Then fish creek is to the left about three hundred yards down the shoreline. It is about one mile paddle from Gene Moler's Point to the narrows. The wild rice is thick in some spots. It varies from year to year. Duck hunting is always good on Nett Lake, because of the wild rice.

Vince Shute and I paddled by Gene Moler's point. We watched flocks of northern and local blue bills fly through the narrows. Just then about eight widgeons flew right by us. I'm pretty deadly with my 36 inch barrel long tom. I said, "Watch this Vince." I aimed about five feet in front of the widgeons at about 100 yards and shot. Two widgeons fell out of the pack.

Vince Shute said, "Well I've seen it so I have to believe it! Nice shot Chavers!"

I said, "Thank you Vince! Just watch me and you will learn something new every day." Vince and I laughed really hard at that one.

He and I paddled up to pick up the two widgeons, but we only found one. The other widgeons must have been crippled and swam away in the thick wild rice.

I said, "Vince, count our ducks." He counted 10. I said, "Let's go up to the narrows and shoot some northern and local blue bills."

Vince Shute said, "Let's do it!"

We paddled out in the open water. Vince shot five local blue bills on our way up to the narrows. Vince and I paddled to the third grass island, next to Fish Creek. Man, the northern and local blue bills were flying kind of high through the narrows. They flew high and about 200 yards out from Fish Creek. Sometimes a few of the local and northern bluebills flew low enough for Vince and me to shoot them.

It was dark and misty out and the clouds were really low. The northern and local blue bills disappeared in the low clouds about 200 yards out from fish creek. Vince shot seven more northern and local blue bills. I shot two northern blue bills.

I said, "Vince, let's paddle over to Ash Point, about ½ mile behind us. There is open water there. I've been watching flocks of mallards fly by Ash Point and they start flying high and disappear in the dark clouds. They are coming from some place behind and around the corner of Ash Point."

I told him, "Vince, look towards Ash Point and you will see for yourself." I pointed in that direction.

He looked towards Ash Point a few minutes then said, "Chavers, I see flocks of mallards coming from behind Ash Point! Chavers, you are the best I know. You watch things. Man, Chavers, you are something else."

Vince Shute and I paddled up to Ash Point. When we got there, I looked at my watch and it was 11:10 a.m. Vince and I threw out the ten mallard decoys and we hid in the thick wild rice next to shore. We did not have to wait long; a flock of black mallards saw our decoys and came flying over them. Vince shot two black mallards with three shots and I shot one black mallard.

We broke for lunch and each of us had a sandwich and a cup of hot coffee. Then five green headed mallards come flying right over the decoys. Vince shot three mallards with three shots.

Watching this, I said, "You are getting better, Vince!" We both laughed hard.

Then he said he could hear geese honking.

I nodded, "I can hear them, too. Look Vince, they are flying low, coming from down towards Wood Duck River; maybe they will land at Nett River." They were snow geese, at least 50 of them. Vince said he could see the white on them.

I said, "They look tired from a long flight, maybe from Canada. If they land at Nett River, we will pick up the mallard decoys and sneak up on them." Sure enough, a few minutes later, they landed at Nett River.

Vince and I picked up the decoys and headed to Nett River where the snow geese landed. Nett River is about ½ mile from Ash Point.

The snow geese must have landed in open water by Nett River. The wild rice was kind of thick, all the way to Nett River. Flocks of mallards and local and northern blue bills flew right over us.

I told Vince Shute not to shoot them; otherwise he would spook the snow geese into flight. Vince nodded OK.

I told him in thirty minutes or less, he could be shooting snow geese. There was a little channel leading into Nett River. It started about a quarter mile out.

I slowly paddled Vince Shute down that channel. We could hear the snow geese making low honks. Vince and I spotted them 150 yards up. By the look of them, I could tell they were very tired. I told Vince I will tell him when to shoot. I also told him, "Try line up two or three of them when you do shoot."

We got about 75 yards away from them. They started to make loud honking noise; I knew they were going to take flight. I said, "Let them have it Vince!" Vince Shute shot two snow geese that lined up together. They both flopped over in the water with their wings spread out. Then the rest all took flight.

I shot a big snow goose. Vince shot two more times and crippled another snow goose; he hit the water with a splash. I ejected my spent shell and quickly put in another three-inch magnum. I shot another snow goose out of the air. Then the snow geese were out of range. Vince Shute finished off the crippled snow goose.

I said, "We killed five snow geese." Vince Shute said, "Jim Chavers, you are the best guide I have ever known. Thank you for the great duck and geese hunt. You are most welcome to hunt or trap on my property any time."

So Vince Shute and I picked up the snow geese and paddled back to Goofies Landing. We had 30 ducks and 5 snow geese. I gave all of them to my friend Vince Shute.

HUNTING PARTRIDGES

Fall 1972 (I was 16)

My mother, Josephine, and I were drinking hot coffee one early Saturday morning. I asked her, "Should I take Wiggie hunting deer, ducks and geese, or partridges today?" Just then a partridge flew past our big picture window toward the graveyard and into the thick woods.

Mother said, "There is your answer—partridges." She motioned, "Look outside, Jim. Wiggie saw the partridge too." Wiggie was looking across the graveyard into the woods.

I went outside and said, "Wiggie, do you want to go hunting partridges?" Wiggie started whining and wagging his tail, still looking across the graveyard into the woods. Then Wiggie came over and stood by my feet, still looking into the woods where the partridge flew. So I petted Wiggie's head and said, "Okay, I'll go get ready."

I went back in the house. Mother said, "Boy, Wiggie sure is anxious to go hunting partridges."

I said, "So am I, Mother." Mother and I looked at each other and laughed really hard.

Then she said, "Get ready. In the meantime I will cook you and Wiggie some egg-and-cheese sandwiches and a thermos of coffee." Mother said, "You know something, Jim, that little dog of yours is smarter than most people."

I said, "Thank you, Mother, I know that!"

It was a nice fall day. I knew there were a lot of ducks and geese out on Nett Lake. It also was the rut mating season for moose and white-tailed deer. There is abundant wildlife in this northern neck of the woods.

While Mother was cooking, I grabbed my Remington three-inch Magnum single-shot Long-Tom shotgun with the 36-inch barrel. I grabbed a couple boxes of six-shot fine shot, and grabbed 10 three-inch Magnum buckshot off my gun rack shelf, in case of deer or moose.

Mother said, "Jim, I put six sandwiches and a thermos of coffee in your backpack." Then she brought my backpack in my bedroom and put it on my bed.

I put my shells in my backpack and told Mother, "Wiggie and I will walk toward Lost River, that way past Woodenfrog's landing. Then I will take the trail toward Lost River, then the trail toward Vince Shute's black bear trail, then to his trailer house. It's about a four-mile walk to Vince Shute's trailer house."

I looked at my watch. The time was 7:05 a.m. I loaded my Long-Tom with six-shot fine shot. I hugged and kissed Mother, and then I put my backpack on. She said, "Good luck, Jim," and followed me out on the porch. She petted Wiggie and said, "You find a lot of partridges for Jim."

Wiggie started whining and jumping around.

I said, "See you later, Mother," and said, "Come on, Wiggie, let's go hunting partridges." Wiggie knew which way to go. He took off running toward the trail to Lost River.

Wiggie was a very smart little dog. He wouldn't go more than 50 yards in front of me. He would sniff all over the ground in every direction until he treed a partridge. He would stop and wait for me until I caught up with him, then he would repeat the same thing over again.

We were on the trail no more than a quarter-mile and Wiggie treed a partridge. I took my backpack off. The partridge was looking down at Wiggie making *weak, weak, weak* noises, teasing Wiggie. I aimed at the partridge's head and shot him. He came flapping his wings down in circles, and Wiggie pounced on him. Wiggie shook the partridge a few times to make sure he was dead and dropped him off at my feet. I said, "Good hunting, Wiggie," and reached down and rubbed his little head.

I loaded my Long-Tom, put the dead partridge in my backpack, put it on, and said, "Find another partridge, Wiggie." Wiggie took off, sniffing the ground in every direction again, looking for partridges.

From mother's house to Woodenfrog's, it was about a one-mile walk through this trail. John Woodenfrog had a trail to his landing on Nett Lake, which was about a one-mile walk. About three-quarters of a mile to John Woodenfrog's Landing, there was a big, rocky, hilly ravine that went for a few miles past Vince Shute's property. The big, hilly, rocky ravines country started about a little over a quarter-mile from

Woodenfrog's landing. On top of this big hill, a trail went to the right and came out at Lost River, which was about a 1½-mile walk. About halfway through this trail to Lost River, there was another trail to the right. It was about a two-mile walk through beautiful hunting country. It came to Vince Shute's black bear trail that led to Lost River from his trailer house. Well, this was the route Wiggie and I were taking. We were going to hit the black bear trail and take it to Vince Shute's trailer house and visit him.

Wiggie and I got to about 200 yards from Woodenfrog's trail that goes to Woodenfrog's landing on Nett Lake. Wiggie treed two more partridges; the third partridge kept flying and disappeared into the thick woods. I took my backpack off to get a better shot at the partridge, but he took off flying. There was only one partridge left. I saw him so I took aim and shot him from about 50 yards away before he took flight. He fell straight down. Wiggie had the dead partridge in his mouth within a second. Wiggie shook him a few times and came and dropped him off at my feet.

Man, I was more than glad I bought this long-range Long-Tom two years ago in the fall of 1970. I had shot a lot of ducks and geese over 100 yards away with this deadly Long-Tom. I had also shot about 15 or 20 huge bucks with buckshot and slugs. I had also shot a big bull moose on the big, hilly, rocky ravines country down by Lost River on Vince Shute's property in the fall of 1971.

I petted Wiggie right after he dropped the second partridge off at my feet. I reloaded my Long-Tom. I put the partridge in my backpack and put it on my back. Then I sicced Wiggie after another partridge again.

We came to Woodenfrog's trail that led to his landing, which was about a half-mile away to the left. Wiggie knew which way to go. We had hunted these woods before. The hilly, rocky ravines country was a little over a quarter-mile to the left. Wiggie and I headed that way. We took a right on the trail that went away from the hilly, rocky ravines country. This trail was very beautiful and abundant with wildlife.

Wiggie and I heard gunshots out on Nett Lake. Somebody was pounding the ducks at Poplar Creek and Swamp Island. Well, duck and geese season opened up next week on October 5th. I was booked full for guiding season. Through this trail there were a lot of white-tailed deer crossings to Lost River, which was about 1½ miles away. Up ahead about a half-mile there was a big open area where cedar loggers cut cedar wood for about a half-mile long and a quarter-mile wide. I had shot a few big bucks with Wiggie in this cedar cutting.

We walked a little over a quarter-mile and two partridges flew up from a big dead log right under Wiggie's nose. They didn't land; they kept flying. Wiggie looked back at me as though he was disgusted, because the partridges kept flying. I said, "It's okay, Wiggie, there will be more." So I called Wiggie back as he was sniffing the ground again.

I sat on the big dead log where the partridges had flown out. I took my backpack off and said to Wiggie, "Do you want a tasty cheese-and-egg sandwich?" I gave Wiggie two sandwiches and I ate two and had a cup of coffee. We sat there for about 20 minutes enjoying the nice fall weather.

Wiggie kept whining and looking toward the cedar cutting. I said, "Wiggie, are there deer at the cedar cutting?" Wiggie jumped up on me with his little paws, looking toward the cedar cutting. So I put in a three-inch Magnum buckshot and put my backpack on and said, "Lead the way, Wiggie."

This time Wiggie didn't go more than 10 feet in front of me. I knew there were deer in the cedar cutting for sure! Wiggie was walking with his little head in the air, sniffing. Usually his little head would be on the ground sniffing.

We got to the edge of the cedar cutting, and sure enough, there were two does and a good-sized buck, standing about 120 yards off, looking the other way. I got butterflies in my stomach. They were upwind from us, so I knew they couldn't smell us. I whispered, "Wiggie, come on, let's go back about 30 yards and sneak up about 50 yards closer, then I will shoot the big buck." Wiggie was smarter than most people. He slowly followed me into the thick cedar woods. I went about 20 yards in and turned right and slowly walked through the cedar woods about 50 yards. Then I slowly and quietly took my backpack off, and Wiggie and I slowly walked to the edge of the cedar woods. I spotted the big buck first, and then I spotted the two does. They were about 75 yards away from Wiggie and me. They were looking right at us, getting ready to run. So I aimed my Long-Tom at the big buck's neck and shot. The big buck fell over dead in his tracks. The two does took off running across the cedar cutting like the devil was after them.

Wiggie went running toward the big buck. I went and grabbed my backpack, reloaded and walked over to the big buck. Wiggie was sniffing the big dead buck. He had six points on one side and five points on the other side, a big 11-point buck. I looked at the buck's neck where I shot him. No doubt the buckshot broke his neck. There were old bullet wounds at the bottom of his chest; it looked like buckshot marks. There was a hard lump right next to his skin. I took my knife out of my backpack and cut the lump open. I found a buckshot pellet. Somebody must have shot this buck last year and he lucked out and lived. Too bad I gunned the big buck down this year with my Long-Tom, thanks to Wiggie. That's why Mother and I know Wiggie is smarter than most people!

I gutted out the big 11-point buck and rubbed deer blood all over Wiggie's cute little face. He likes that! Now the noisy ravens would have a lot of deer guts to fight over. I dragged the big buck by his antlers into the woods to a big oak tree with a low-hanging branch. I took a rope out of my backpack, tied it around the buck's antlers, threw the rope around the thick branch, and hoisted the big buck in the air until his back legs were touching the ground. I would borrow Vince Shute's three-wheel trail rider and come get the big buck before nightfall. Two noisy ravens already smelled the buck's blood. They flew in circles, making all kinds of weird noises, and landed in the oak trees about 200 yards away. They would leave the big buck alone while he was hanging and eat the gut pile on the ground.

I looked at my watch. The time was 10:17 a.m. Wiggie was sniffing around in the brush not far off. I said, "Come on, Wiggie; let's go find some more partridges." Wiggie took off toward the trail, sniffing the ground in every direction toward Lost River. Wiggie waited for me to catch up. About a little over a quarter-mile we came to the trail that led to Vince Shute's black bear trail, which was about two miles away. Wiggie and I took a right turn and Wiggie treed two partridges. I took my backpack off and walked to where Wiggie was sniffing the ground, and then looking up in the tree. I saw a spruce hen looking down at Wiggie and me. The spruce hens are considered dumber than the partridge, which is true. I aimed my Long-Tom at the spruce hen's head and shot. He came flapping down in circles and almost landed in Wiggie's mouth. The other spruce hen flew to another tree and landed. They are no doubt dumber than partridges.

Wiggie dropped the dead hen by my feet. I loaded my Long-Tom and aimed at the second spruce hen from about 50 yards away and shot. He came flapping down in circles and hit the ground. Wiggie was on him in about a split second, shaking the dead spruce hen. Then Wiggie brought the second spruce hen over and dropped him at my feet while I was loading my Long-Tom. I said, "Good hunting, Wiggie," and reached down and patted his little side. Wiggie started licking my hand. He looked cute and crazy with the dried deer blood all over his cute little face. I put the two spruce hens in my backpack with the two partridges and said, "Come on, Wiggie, find some more partridges." Wiggie took off down the trail toward Vince Shute's black bear trail, sniffing the ground in every direction.

We got to the most beautiful scenery in this neck of the woods. In the fall the oak, poplar, maple, and birch leaves turn beautiful red, yellow, and orange. It looked like they went for miles in every direction.

Then all of a sudden out of a gully came a huge male black bear. Wiggie started barking and running around the black bear. The black bear stood up on his hind legs, and I hollered at Wiggie to come over by me and leave the black bear alone. Wiggie came next to me. The big male black bear sniffed the air a few times, got down on all fours, and went about his business, slowly walking in the beautiful woods. That big male black bear was one of Vince Shute's pet black bears. I had seen him at Vince Shute's trailer house before with a few other black bears.

Wiggie and I slowly walked toward Vince Shute's black bear trail, which was about one mile away, Wiggie sniffing the ground in every direction. Wiggie and I got on the black bear trail that led to Lost River and Vince Shute's trailer house, which was about a half-mile away. Wiggie ran in the thick woods, sniffing. Two partridges took flight and landed in the trees, looking down at Wiggie. I could see one partridge from where I stood about 25 to 30 yards away. He started making *weak, weak, weak* noises. I quickly took my backpack off, aimed my Long-Tom at his head, and shot. The partridge came flapping down in circles. Wiggie was on him in an instant, shaking the partridge to make sure he was dead. I quickly reloaded my Long-Tom, but the second partridge flew off in the thick woods to live to see another day. Wiggie dropped the dead partridge off at my feet. I said, "Good hunting, Wiggie," and reached down and petted him. I put the partridge in my backpack and said, "Come on, Wiggie, let's go visit Vince Shute."

I looked at my watch. The time was 12:08 p.m. Then Wiggie took off, sniffing the ground in every direction, toward Vince Shute's. Wiggie and I got to about a quarter-mile away from Vince Shute's and Wiggie treed a big male fisher. Wiggie and I looked at the fisher for a few minutes, and I said, "Come on, Wiggie, I will trap him this winter." So Wiggie and I headed to Vince Shute's trailer house.

As we got close, I called Wiggie over to me in case Vince Shute was outside feeding some black bears. Nobody was in sight, not even a black bear. Vince Shute must be inside his trailer house. I knocked and within a few seconds Vince Shute came to the door and said, "By God, its Jim Chavers and his good little hunting dog, Wiggie. Come on in and have a cup of hot coffee and donuts. " Wiggie followed me inside and Vince Shute said, "I have a few donuts for the best little hunting dog in the world too." Vince Shute reached down and petted Wiggie.

I took my backpack off and set it under Vince Shute's table. Vince Shute poured me a cup of hot coffee and said, "I see you have your Long-Tom along. What are you and Wiggie hunting in my neck of the woods?"

I said, "Wiggie and I were hunting partridges, and I came by this big eleven-point buck and I shot him. "

Vince Shute said, "I bet your little dog Wiggie let you know the buck was there. "

I said, "He sure did."

Vince Shute said, "Well, there you go. Wiggie is smarter than most people."

"That's what Mother and I said."

Vince Shute threw Wiggie a donut. Wiggie caught the donut in mid-air. Vince Shute asked, "Wiggie has dried blood on his cute little face?"

I said, "That's dried deer blood. When I gut a deer, I rub the blood all over Wiggie's cute little face. He likes that."

Vince Shute said, "Well, I'll be damned."

Then he asked, "Did you shoot any partridges?"

I said, "Yes I did, three partridges and two spruce hens."

I added, "I'll tell you what: I will give you two spruce hens and half of the eleven-point buck if you let Wiggie and me use your trail rider to go get the buck." I handed Vince Shute the old buckshot pellet I dug out of the buck's chest and said, "This goes with the deal."

Vince Shute started laughing and said, "Deal," while he was looking at the buckshot pellet.

Then Vince said, "After you drink your coffee, we will go to my big shed and you can warm it up and drive it out."

I drank my coffee, and then took a few six-shot fine shot and five three-inch Magnum buckshot out of my backpack. I left my backpack under the table with Vince Shute. I said, "After I tie the big buck in back of your trail rider, I will drive to Mother's house and have her follow me back here to your trailer house for a ride home."

Vince Shute said, "Good thinking. Then I can have a cup of coffee with your mother."

I finished my coffee, and then Wiggie and I followed Vince outside. Vince Shute looked around to make sure there were no black bears in sight. Wiggie would have let us both know if there were any black bears around. We followed Vince Shute over to his big shed. He had three red sheds. Vince Shute opened his big shed door and said, "There you go, Chavers, have at it."

I let the trail rider warm up for a few minutes, and Wiggie started growling, looking toward the woods. There stood the big male black bear that Wiggie and I had encountered back in the woods. I related the story to Vince Shute in a few minutes.

Then I said, "Come on, Wiggie." Wiggie jumped up on my lap and we headed down that old black bear trail toward Lost River. My Long-Tom stuck out a little bit on Vince Shute's built-in gun rack on his trail rider, but it would hold.

As Wiggie and I got within 200 yards of the big buck, we could see 15 to 20 noisy ravens eating on the gut pile. As we got closer they all took flight, making all kinds of weird noises. Some circled, others landed in trees not far off. The deer gut pile was half gone; it didn't take the ravens long to devour half the gut pile. They did not touch the big buck, but after the gut pile was gone, then they would have started to eat on the big buck.

I cut the rope and the big buck fell down. I tied the big buck on the back of Vince Shute's trail rider. Wiggie was sniffing what was left of the gut pile. I said, "Come on, Wiggie; let's let the noisy ravens have what's left of the gut pile." So Wiggie came running and jumped up on my lap, and we slowly rode toward Mother's house.

I pulled up in Mother's yard. She was out on the porch, sitting in her rocking chair, enjoying the nice fall weather. Wiggie jumped down and went running around Mother's house to go investigate his territory. Wiggie always did that when we came home from a hunting trip. Mother said, "You went hunting partridges and you came back with a nice big buck."

So I told Mother the whole story. I told her, "Vince Shute wants to drink a cup of coffee with you."

She said, "Okay, I will go in the house and get ready."

I said, "In the meantime, I will put the big buck in back of your truck."

Then Wiggie came back from checking his territory out. I went in the house and told Mother that Wiggie and I would meet her at Vince Shute's. She said, "Tell him I will be out there in about half an hour."

I said, "I will do that, Mother."

I went back outside and said, "Wiggie, let's go back to Vince Shute's and Mother will pick us up." Wiggie jumped up in my lap and we rode down one side of the road on the main highway. We got to the reservation line, which was about three miles from Mother's. There was an old, weaving logging road to the left that was about 1½ miles to Vince Shute's trailer house. About one mile through this old logging road to the right, there is a big rock that went about 10-15 feet in the air. There is also a big beaver dam a little over a quarter-mile in the woods toward the main highway from the big rock.

I looked at my watch. The time was 3:47 p.m. So Wiggie and I went about 300 yards down the old logging road, and three partridges took flight right on the edge of the road. They landed in the trees not far off the old gravel road. I didn't even get to stop. Wiggie jumped and went rolling in the dust and tall grass. He got up and went and stopped under the tree where one of the partridges landed. I busted out laughing really hard. At least Wiggie was okay. Boy, Wiggie sure got excited when it came to hunting partridges—or anything for that matter. Well, I get excited too.

Wiggie was wagging his tail, looking up in the tree at the partridge. I shut the trail rider off. I could see the partridge looking down at Wiggie from about 30 feet up in a birch tree. I took aim at his head and shot. The partridge flew around in circles, slowly coming down. When he got to about five feet off the ground, Wiggie made a running jump and snatched the partridge out of the air. Then Wiggie shook the partridge a few times to make sure he was dead, and came and dropped him off at my feet.

Wiggie started looking around in the trees again. I had already reloaded my Long-Tom. The other two partridge both took flight at the same time. I looked down at Wiggie and said, "Good hunting, Wiggie. Are you all right?" I reached down and picked up poor little Wiggie and looked his little body over to make sure he was okay. Wiggie seemed to be okay so I reached down, grabbed the partridge, put him in the inside of my jacket pocket, and started the trail rider up. I said, "Come on, Wiggie; let's head to Vince Shute's." Wiggie jumped up on my lap and we headed down the old logging trail.

By the time Wiggie and I got to Vince Shute's trailer house, Mother's brown Chevy truck was backed up to Vince Shute's big red shed. He had the big buck hoisted up in the air and half skinned already. Vince Shute said, "Ms. Chavers, there are the best two hunters in this neck of the woods."

Mother was drinking a cup of hot coffee. I reached inside my jacket and took the partridge out and handed it to Vince Shute. He said, "Thank you, Chavers and Wiggie."

I said, "I will go in your trailer house and get my backpack and give you the two spruce hens. "

Mother said, "I grabbed it and it's in the back of the truck."

So I grabbed my backpack, opened it, and took the two spruce hens out and handed them to Vince Shute. I said, "Now, Mother, there are three partridges for you, and one partridge and two spruce hens for Vince Shute."

Vince Shute said, "And half a deer if I get done skinning it and cutting it up."

All of a sudden Wiggie started growling over by the edge of the woods. I hollered, "Come here, Wiggie, before a black bear gets you."

Mother said, "Oh no, I'm going to get in the truck."

Wiggie came and stood by my feet, looking into the woods. Vince said, "Probably one of my black bears. He must smell the deer's blood."

Vince Shute got the hide off and used his axe and hand saw to finish the deer. Wiggie and I did not see any black bear, but Wiggie knew he was in the area someplace. Vince put half of the deer in one of his tubs and I helped him carry it to the back of Mother's truck. Mother said, "Thank you for the coffee, and it was nice visiting you."

Vince said, "Same to you, Ms. Chavers, and come visit more often."

Mother started up her truck, and I said, "Come on, Wiggie." He jumped up in the truck. I told Vince I would bring his tub back tomorrow. We shook hands and I got in the truck, and we headed for home.

TRAPPING STORY

November 1972. Trapping in Vince Shute's backyard.

I planned to set traps for fisher, fox, beaver and muskrats and I took along some rotten food and wire. That November, I took five fisher traps, five fox traps, five beaver traps and five muskrat traps and brought my ax. I had three egg sandwiches and a thermos of coffee. My back pack was full; it weighed close to 60 pounds. My mother Josephine let me off at 7:30 a.m., same place as the day before. I put on my snowshoes, grabbed my back pack and I grabbed my 22 magnum then took off walking towards Vince Shute's on the old logging road.

I walked close to ½ a mile and two deer tracks walked on top of yesterday's snowshoe tracks. They walked on top of my tracks for about 100 yards, then they headed into a cedar woods. There is a lot of wildlife in these cedar woods on Vince Shute's property. To name a few: black bear, timber wolves, white tailed deer, fisher, lynx or bob cat, mink, martin, wood chucks, weasel, otter, beaver, muskrats, fox, rabbits, grouse, red squirrel, and all kinds of different hawks, birds of prey.

I walked another ½ mile down the old logging road towards Vince Shute's. I could see the huge rock off in the distance.

The big beaver dam was about ½ mile back in the woods. I took a ten minute break. I sat on a huge stump and had a cup of coffee.

As I was sitting there enjoying my coffee, I watched a mink dig in the three feet of snow; he was hunting for a meal, maybe a field mouse or something. Then he ran and disappeared in the thick woods.

I drank up my coffee and headed towards the big beaver dam. There were all kinds of old and fresh deer tracks in the deep snow. I could see the big beaver dam off in the distance. I got there and could see three beaver houses. I also noticed where a fisher crossed to the other side of the beaver dam on the fresh snow.

There were all kinds of wildlife tracks on top of the three feet of snow and frozen ice. There were fresh fox tracks all over the beaver dams. Maybe I could catch a fisher, beaver, and fox and muskrat trapping in this big beaver dam.

My watch said it was 10:15 a.m. I walked right up to a big beaver house; it was next to a muskrat house, and there were two muskrat houses in the big beaver dam. I could hear the beaver inside the beaver house. I took off my snowshoes then my back pack.

I took my ax out and chopped a hole through the ice, right on side of the beaver dam. I did the same thing on the other side of the beaver dam. I put a beaver trap in each hole; I put the trap on a pole, so the beaver, if I caught one, would drown his/her self.

Since the muskrat house was close by, I chopped a hole on top of the muskrat house and set a trap inside the muskrat house. Then I covered the hole with parts of the muskrat house and light snow.

I walked across to another big beaver dam. I chopped a hole right next to the beaver dam. I did the same thing to the next beaver dam.

There was a muskrat house on the edge of the beaver dam. I chopped a hole on top of the muskrat house and did the same thing as I did to the first muskrat house. I had one beaver trap left and three muskrat traps left.

I walked to the edge of the beaver dam where I saw the fisher tracks in the snow. I put rotten food on the fisher trap. I set out three fisher traps along the tree line where the fisher ran. I hoped to catch a fisher. I thought, *I'll check all my traps early tomorrow morning.* I set out five fox traps, all along the beaver dam. I also put rotten food on the fox traps and tied the fox traps down with wire.

Now it was 3:30 p.m. It would take me a little over an hour and a half to get back out to the main highway. I would catch a ride home with someone from Nett Lake. I took off walking and got out to the road at 5:15 p.m. I caught a ride home with one of my friends as soon as I got out to the road.

Back at home, I told my mother how many traps I set. I told her, "In the morning, I will go back and check my traps."

Up early the next morning, we had breakfast together, and my mother drove me out to the Nett Lake Indian Reservation line and dropped me off. It was 7:15 a.m. I had my back pack and my 22 magnum in case I had to kill one of the animals. I told my mother to pick me up at around 10:00 a.m. I put my snowshoes on, back pack, and I walked down the old logging road, towards Vince Shute's again.

As I got close to the huge rock, I saw two timber wolves take off running. They must have been watching me as I was walking towards them. I got too close for their comfort and they ran away. What a wonderful sight it is to watch two timber wolf run through the deep snow; it's an awesome sight.

I sat down on a big stump, resting, and had a cup of coffee. Two ravens flew over me, making noise. They were dive-bombing each other. The big beaver dam was not far away. I followed yesterday's snowshoe tracks to the big beaver dam.

Right away I spotted a fox caught in one of my traps. The fox was trying desperately to get away. I walked up to the fox and shot him in back of the head, to put the fox out of his misery. I then took the fox's leg out of the trap and put the fox and trap in my back pack.

I checked all five of my fisher traps but I had no luck with the fisher trapping. I put the five fisher traps in my back pack.

I walked over to the muskrat house next to the big beaver dam. I checked the muskrat house first, and sure enough, I caught a muskrat. So I shot the muskrat in back of the head. I put the muskrat and trap in back of my back pack; I did not leave any traps behind.

I had to break the ice away and then I checked the beaver traps. I found one drown beaver in one trap, but no beaver in the other trap. The beaver was big and heavy, close to 50 pounds. I would have to make two trips out to the road if I caught another beaver. I put both beaver traps in my back pack and I left the beaver to lay on the snow and ice.

I walked over to the other muskrat house and sure enough, I had another muskrat caught in the trap. So I shot the muskrat in back of the head. Then I put him in back of my back pack. I had one fox and two muskrats in back of my back pack.

I walked over to the other big beaver house, I had to break the ice away and sure enough, I had another drowned beaver; I had three beaver, one fox, two muskrats and no fisher. Not bad for a day's trapping.

I looked at my watch and it was 10:35 a.m. I knew my mother was on time to pick me up, but this wasn't the first time I was late (and it won't be the last time either.) I left my backpack off on the snowshoe trail that led out to the road. It was heavy with traps, one fox, and two muskrats. Then I walked over to the beaver house and brought the beaver over to my backpack. Then I did the same thing with the other two beavers. Carrying two beaver at the same time with snow shoes on is very heavy. I made two trips out to the main highway.

Waawaashkeshiinh

(White tailed Deer)
(wa-wa-shkay-she)

By Charles Grolla

The white tailed deer is the most hunted animal of the Ojibwe nowadays and there are many uses for the deer's body parts besides just the meat.

The deer's antlers were used not only for its medicinal uses but they were used for hauling sweat lodge rocks from the fire pit to the sweat lodge. The male deer what is usually referred to a "big buck" also has its own Ojibwe name "eyaabe" (aye-yaw-bay) and this means a big buck and can be used for the big antlered males of the white tailed deer, elk, and caribou species.

When hunted and a kill is made, the first thing done is an offering of tobacco, made at the kill site. If it is male, the male genitalia is separated during field dressing and is hung in a nearby tree. This is to pay respect to the male deer's responsibility to reproduce and it is said it is too help ensure that more deer are to come and there will be many deer in the future.

The hooves of the deer were traditionally used for male dance outfits like the dance outfits worn at pow wows; these deer hooves have been replaced nowadays with bells but you can still see some dancers using the old style of leg wear of traditional white tailed deer hooves. They encompass the leg near the upper calf of the leg and many deer hooves are tanned and layered around the dancer's leg and when the dancer steps to the beat of the drum, the hooves make a distinct sound. The men's traditional dancer is the only style dancer that uses the old style hooves instead of bells. The deer's hide is preferred in the summer time for use of making drums because the deer's hide is thinner and has less hair and is easier to turn into rawhide for the drums.

The spotted fawn hides are used for the bundle used for babies to keep the dried umbilical cord when it falls off, a lock of hair from the baby's first haircut, among other sacred things while a child grows up and is kept as kind of sentimental keepsake for this person, and it has spiritual power. When a male makes his first deer kill, it is seen as the marker in life between childhood and manhood and this first kill of a deer ceremony is a bit more elaborate and is understood as an introduction into manhood and the responsibilities that go with being a man in the community and in the home.

After the kill and the processing of the meat and the rest of the deer's body, the deer's legs and head are taken out in the woods and placed and tied together in a tree about shoulder high in the branches of a tree near the trunk and ribbons are hung from them and tobacco placed on the ground at the bottom of the tree.

This is how respect is given to the deer as thanks and appreciation of the deer giving and blessing the hunter and his family with the meat and items from the deer's body. The White tailed deer is a clan but is not numerous in the area I reside.

WHITE-TAILED DEER HUNTING STORY

Late October 1972

It was an early fall morning. The rut mating season for Bull Moose and white-tailed deer was on. I told my mother, Josephine, instead of taking Wiggie hunting ducks and geese, I would take Wiggie hunting deer on the other side of Vince Shute's property.

Mother said, "Jim that will be good. We have enough ducks in the freezer. We can use some deer meat."

I said, "Okay. After I drink my coffee, I will go get ready."

Besides, Vince Shute had told me he hired some of his logger friends to cut down about a quarter-mile of his cedar wood on the other side of his road, toward the Rabbit Lake Road toward Orr, Minnesota. Vince also told me there was another big rock that went about 10 feet in the air to sit on. It was on the edge of the cedar cutting about one mile from his trailer house.

"You can walk to the big rock from the Rabbit Lake Road or from my trailer house," Vince Shute said. "Chavers, as you well know, it's abundant with wildlife on my property. I know you will kill a deer or two. Just bring me some deer meat; that is all I ask. Besides, you are the only one I let hunt on my property." Vince Shute told me all this about his land back in 1968, when I first met him, when I brought him ducks off Nett Lake.

I looked at the clock on Mother's wall. It read 7:15 a.m. I told Mother, "I will go outside and tell Wiggie not to go anyplace. We are going hunting white-tailed deer on Vince Shute's property. Maybe we will kill that big Bull Moose Milo and John Day saw cross the road yesterday by the Rabbit Lake Road. He headed toward Vince Shute's property. Milo and John were going to Farmer John's Landing on Pelican Lake for some fishing. They ran out of sucker minnows. They took the back way to Orr, Minnesota, to buy more sucker minnows. That's when they saw him."

I had let Wiggie outside early in the morning to go relieve himself and check his territory out. I could see Wiggie from Mother's big sliding picture window. He started scratching on the back door to come inside. I taught Wiggie that when he was growing up back in 1968. I went outside and told Wiggie that we were going hunting white-tailed deer on Vince Shute's property. He started whining and jumping around. Wiggie loves hunting, trapping, and even fishing. I petted little cute Wiggie and rubbed his sides and ears. Wiggie followed me back in the house.

Mother said, "Wiggie sure is a smart little dog."

I said, "Smarter than most people."

Wiggie followed me into our bedroom. I had built a little wooden box for Wiggie since he was a little pup back in 1968. Mother hollered, "Jim, I will make you and Wiggie some egg-and-cheese sandwiches and a thermos of coffee."

I hollered back, "Thank you, Mother."

I had a good collection of deer rifles and pistols: a bolt-action .270 Savage with a high-powered scope; a bolt-action .30-06 Remington with a high-powered scope; an automatic .30-06 Remington Magnum with a high-powered scope; a bolt-action .30-06 Sears with a high-powered scope; an automatic .30-06 Savage with peep sight; a lever-action; 30-30 Marlin with peep sight; a bolt-action .300 Weatherby Magnum with a high-powered scope; and a bolt-action .22 Winchester Magnum with a scope.

I also had two bolt-action .22 Rugers with peep sight and a .22 automatic Ruger rifle.

The shotguns I owned: a 12-gauge Remington Long-Tom 36-inch barrel single-shot for long range on ducks and geese; a 12-gauge Remington pump 3-inch Magnum; a 12-gauge Remington automatic 3-inch Magnum; and a 12-gauge 3-inch Sears pump gun.

Now pistols: .22 Magnum automatic target; .357 Magnum revolver; .44 Magnum revolver; .45 1911 automatic; P40 Tarus automatic; .50 Desert Eagle automatic; .50 Magnum Colt revolver; .454 Magnum 5-shot revolver.

I said, "Wiggie, which gun should I use?" as though I was talking to another human. "Since we will be sitting on top of a big rock, I usually use my automatic Remington 30-06 rifle with a high-powered scope. This time I will use my bolt-action .300 Weatherby Magnum with a high-powered scope." So I took it off one of my gun racks on the wall.

Then I heard cawing at my bedroom window. I had three pet crows and one of them was begging for food. Then the other two crows came and landed on a board I had put there for them to sit on by my window. Soon all three were cawing for me to feed them. So I went in the kitchen and my mother said, "I hear your pet crows. You better feed them. There are some hot dogs in the package in the refrigerator."

I said, "Yes, Mother," so I took the hot dogs, opened my window, and fed my three pet crows. I also gave Wiggie two hot dogs. The three crows flew toward my brother Duze Chavers' house. Crows are good pets. Every spring I get a few crows for pets. Wiggie doesn't bother them.

Mother brought four egg-and-cheese sandwiches and a thermos of coffee into my bedroom. I said, "Thank you, Mother."

She said, "Looks like you are almost ready to go. I will go warm up that old truck. "

I put my Nikon binoculars in my backpack, also the four sandwiches and thermos of coffee. I loaded my .300 Weatherby Magnum, and then I put the shells in a side pocket on my backpack. Then I said, "Let's go hunting deer, Wiggie." He ran to the back door.

We stepped out into a nice, calm October day. It would be a good day for hunting deer or Bull Moose. My brother Duze was standing by the truck talking to Mother. Wiggie and I walked over to the truck.

Duze said, "I just came from Orr, Minnesota about a half-hour ago. A big buck ran right out in front of me. I had to slam on the brakes so I wouldn't hit him. He ran in the woods toward Vince Shute's property. I was just walking over to tell you, Jim, but I see you are going hunting deer."

I said, "Yes, I'm going hunting deer on the east side, the road by Vince Shute's property, by the Rabbit Lake Road that way."

Duze said, "Good. I know you will shoot a deer or two. I will cut him up and skin him out for you, if I can keep the deer hide."

I said, "That's a deal."

I looked at my watch. The time was 8:03 a. m. Wiggie and I had all day to hunt deer. It started getting dark about 6:20 p.m. I told Mother to pick Wiggie and me up at around 6:00 p.m., just before dark, on the Rabbit Lake Road where she let us off. She said, "Okay, let's get going." Duze walked back to his house. I put my backpack in back of the truck, then I told Wiggie to jump in the back, and Mother drove out of the yard.

The Rabbit Lake Road where Wiggie and I would be hunting deer was about six or seven miles from Mother's house. Vince Shute's trailer house was about four miles from Mother's house. Wiggie had his paws up on the edge of Mother's truck, looking and sniffing the air in every direction. Wiggie was surely by far the best and cutest little hunting dog I'd ever have! He could retrieve every duck and goose I shot, no matter how cold the water was. He would let me know which way the deer were coming from. If it wasn't for Wiggie, I wouldn't bring half the game home that I did.

We got by the reservation line, which was three miles from our house, and two does ran across the road right in front of us. Wiggie saw them and ran to the other side of Mother's truck, watching them. The two does ran toward Vince Shute's property. Mother got excited; so did I.

I said, "Stop the truck and back up. Where there are does, there are bucks." So Mother stopped and backed up, then stopped where the two does ran in the woods toward Vince Shute's. Wiggie was sniffing the air for about three minutes, but no buck came out.

I told Mother to take off driving, which she did. Besides, Vince Shute's road was about one mile up ahead to the left on a big corner, and Farmer John's road was about 200 yards farther to the left, where we were going. We went past Vince Shute's driveway and took a left turn on Farmer John's road. Pelican Lake is three miles down this curvy road. About three-quarters of the way, there is a gravel road to the left—that is the Rabbit Lake Road to Orr, Minnesota. This is a very curvy gravel road. It went about five miles, then it came to a sharp corner to the right, and then it went about five more miles and came to Highway 53. To the right went to Orr, Minnesota; to the left went to International Falls, Minnesota.

We got to the Rabbit Lake Road and took a left turn. Before we got to the sharp corner, which was about five miles away, there were three old curvy logging roads that went toward Vince Shute's property. At the sharp corner there was a road to the left that went to Lost River. This big area is abundant with wildlife, mostly white-tailed deer. It is also abundant for trapping fur animals. The cedar wood loggers were in the second logging road to the left, about 1 3/4 mile in. The loggers were not cutting cedar wood today. All the way through this big area, down past

Lost River, there are open areas about ¼ miles wide, good for hunting white-tailed deer and Bull Moose. About two years ago a non-Indian deer hunter shot an 18-point, over 300 pounds, swamp buck down this road by Lost River. I saw the swamp buck myself. He was massive.

I told Mother to let Wiggie and me off at the second old logging road to Vince Shute's property. She stopped and let Wiggie and me off and wished us good luck on our deer hunting trip. I got butterflies in my stomach. I told Mother to pick us up at 6:00 p.m. Wiggie was already sniffing the ground and making grunting and snorting noises. Mother said, "Wiggie sure is excited!"

I grabbed my deer-slayer bolt-action .300 Weatherby Magnum, put my backpack on, and said, "See you this afternoon, Mother."

She said, "I will be here waiting for you and Wiggie," and drove off to home.

I looked at my watch. The time was 9:12 a. m. I said, "Lead the way, Wiggie." He took off zigzagging down the old logging road, sniffing the ground in every direction. Wiggie would go about 50 yards in front of me, then he would stop, look back, and wait for me to catch up to him, then he would take off, sniffing the ground in every direction again. I taught Wiggie to wait until I caught up to him when he was about a year old. When Wiggie knew there were deer up ahead, he would stop with his little ears sticking up in the direction the deer were standing.

This is beautiful and very good deer hunting land. No wonder Vince Shute bought all this land. It had lots of hills and all kinds of different trees. It had open areas with clumps of trees here and there.

Vince Shute sure knew what he was doing when he bought this land over 50 years ago.

Wiggie and I walked a little over a quarter-mile, and Wiggie scared up two partridges. They both kept flying. Wiggie was running from tree to tree, looking for the partridges. Wiggie was looking back at me as though I was supposed to shoot a partridge. I said, "That's okay, Wiggie. I get excited too, but we are hunting deer, not partridges." Wiggie seemed to understand. I said, "Lead the way, Wiggie," so he took off down the old logging road, sniffing the ground in every direction. He stopped a few times and looked back, but Wiggie kept going. He must have been thinking about the two partridges; that's why he stopped and looked back.

We got three-quarters of a mile down the old logging road, and I saw Wiggie standing there with his little ears sticking up. Right away I knew Wiggie saw or knew there were deer up ahead. I stopped and took my backpack off for a better shot. Then I slowly tiptoed up to Wiggie and looked in the direction he was looking. Sure enough, about 300 yards across an opening by the edge of a clump of birch trees on a hill, a big buck and three does were standing there looking at Wiggie and me. So I put my crosshairs on the big buck's neck and shot. The bullet from the powerful .300 Weatherby Magnum broke the big buck's neck. He fell over backwards and died in his tracks. The three does took off running over the hill like the devil was after them and disappeared in the thick woods. Wiggie ran up to the big buck.

I walked back, put my backpack on and walked up to the big buck and Wiggie. I said, "Good hunting, Wiggie," as I leaned my .300

Weatherby Magnum up against a birch tree and took my backpack off. I reached down and rubbed Wiggie's cute little head as he was sniffing the big buck's bloody neck. I counted six points on the left side and five points on the right side; it was a big 11-point buck that weighed close to 250 pounds with the guts in him. I took my knife out and started gutting the big buck. I said, "Wiggie, come here." I grabbed little Wiggie and rubbed blood all over little Wiggie's cute head and face. Wiggie stood there licking the blood off his face and little paws.

Then two noisy ravens circled us, investigating our kill. Soon there would be more of them. I took a nylon rope out of my backpack, tied it around the big buck's antlers, and dragged him 50 feet to the closest oak tree. Then I threw the rope around the lowest branch about 10 feet up and hoisted the big buck as far off the ground as I could get him, which wasn't far. Good enough for the blood to drain out of him. The noisy ravens would devour the gut pile first, then they would start on the big buck next, but I planned on coming to get the big buck later this afternoon, most likely at dark.

I made sure there was a bullet in my .300 Weatherby Magnum, and then leaned it against the birch tree. I put my backpack on, grabbed my rifle, and said, "Come on, Wiggie, let's go find that big rock at the cedar cutting." Again Wiggie went sniffing the ground in every direction down the old logging road. There were a lot of deer tracks crossing the road in the mud. Wiggie and I walked about a half-mile more, and Wiggie stopped up ahead in the middle of the road. He was sniffing something. When I got up to where Wiggie was, he was sniffing some huge old Bull Moose tracks. I could tell they were two-to-three-day-old tracks, and they crossed the old logging road. Maybe with luck I would get the chance to shoot him from on top of the big rock, since it was mating season. I said, "Wiggie, we must be on Vince Shute's property by now." The old logging road was muddy in places from all the logging trucks. I said, "Lead the way, Wiggie." He took off sniffing the ground in every direction.

We went about quarter-mile and Wiggie stopped again with his little ears sticking up. I said to myself, *Deer*, so I took my backpack off and slowly tiptoed up to Wiggie. Then all of a sudden two does took off running. All I saw was their white tails waving good-bye. I looked all over for a buck but there was none. I said, "Good hunting, Wiggie," and reached down and rubbed his little head.

We both walked back to my backpack. I put it on and said, "Let's go find that cedar cutting and that big rock." I figured Wiggie and I walked at least 1½ miles so far. From the Rabbit Lake Road where Wiggie and I got off through the woods, it should be about three miles or so to Vince Shute's trailer house. Wiggie and I walked around two corners. An old cedar cutting was on both sides of the old logging road.

Wiggie stopped up ahead on the road and was sniffing something. When I walked up to Wiggie, he was sniffing the huge Bull Moose tracks again. This time the Bull Moose tracks were about one day old, and he had crossed the road and headed toward Lost River. I reached down and petted little Wiggie's head. He started licking my hand. I said, "Wiggie, that big Bull Moose must have crossed Lost River and went up in those big rocky hills."

Wiggie started whining and his little ears were sticking up; he was looking on the other side of the old logging road by the birch and cedar woods. I looked and saw three does standing about 200 yards away. They were looking at Wiggie and me, but I didn't see any bucks. The three does took off running and jumping at the same time and disappeared into the thick woods. I said, "Wiggie, it sure would be easy shooting does, but we are hunting bucks and Bull Moose."

I looked at my watch. Now it said 12:07 p.m. There were a lot of fresh deer tracks in the mud crossing this old logging road. Wiggie and I stopped for a few minutes to listen. Then three noisy ravens flew right over us, making all kinds of weird noises. They did that when they smelled blood. They were heading in the direction of the big buck I shot, most likely after the gut pile. Wiggie's little ears were sticking up, and he was looking down the old logging road. We were on another straight stretch, a little less than a quarter-mile, and then a sharp corner. A big buck with a massive rack of horns came running out of the cedar woods and ran around the sharp corner. I could smell the fresh cedar wood. I could tell the cedar cutting started up at the corner. His rack of horns was bigger and wider than the big 11-point buck I shot.

I got excited. I had butterflies in my stomach. Wiggie and I slowly walked up to the corner where the cedar cutting started. Wiggie found the big buck's running tracks in the mud on the side of the old logging road. Wiggie started sniffing the huge buck's tracks, and we followed them around the corner. I spotted the big rock about 300 yards up ahead on the left side of the old logging road. As Wiggie and I followed the huge buck's tracks, he had run down the side of the road 100 yards and took a right turn, ran out in the cedar cutting and disappeared in the thick woods. On the right side of the road, the loggers cut cedar wood about 200 yards back, then on the left side about the same distance they cut cedar wood. There were rows of cedar logs on both sides of the old logging road. The big rock was on the edge of the cedar cutting by the old logging road, just like Vince Shute said it would be.

Wiggie and I walked up to the big rock. It went between 10 and 15 feet in the air. The little old logging road kept going, most likely toward Vince Shute's trailer house. I could tell from on top of the big rock you would be able to see really well. It was another good spot for hunting white-tailed deer and Bull Moose. There were two different ways to climb up on the big rock, so I climbed up first, and then I called Wiggie. He came running and jumping up the big rock with no problem. I thought Wiggie was part squirrel for a minute there.

Man, we could see well almost in every direction. This big rock was just like the big rock a half-mile on the west side of Vince Shute's trailer house, toward the Nett Lake Indian Reservation line. I took my backpack off. Wiggie and I sat there for about 20 minutes, enjoying Mother Nature's beautiful scenery. Wiggie was looking in the air, so I looked up and saw two bald eagles were circling beautifully. The Indian way, when you see eagles circling it means good medicine. So I took my binoculars out of my backpack, then Wiggie and I watched the eagles circle the beautiful sky for about five minutes. They must have seen the noisy ravens eating on the gut pile. Then both eagles dove down toward Pelican Lake that way.

I opened my backpack and took out four egg-and-cheese sandwiches and my thermos of coffee. I gave Wiggie two egg-and-cheese sandwiches and I ate my two egg-and-cheese sandwiches with coffee.

Then Wiggie's ears went up. He was staring down the old logging road the way we came. I looked and a big male black bear was following Wiggie's and my tracks. As the big male black bear got closer, I could hear Wiggie's little low growl in his chest. I whispered, "Wiggie, stop growling, he won't bother us. I've got this .300 Weatherby Magnum; we are on top of this big rock. Wiggie quit growling. "

The big male black bear was one of Vince Shute's pets. The big male black bear got to where Wiggie and I were. He walked around the big rock, sniffing. He knew Wiggie and I were on top of the big rock. Then he looked up at us for a few seconds, and then he headed down that old logging road toward Vince Shute's trailer house. He must have smelled us and our egg-and-cheese sandwiches.

I looked at my watch. The time was 1:15 p.m. Wiggie and I waited and watched for about another 30 minutes. Then Wiggie's ears went up. He was staring in the direction where the big massive buck ran into the woods. I looked and two does were standing at the edge of the cedar woods, eating. I got butterflies in my stomach. The two does must have been eating the cedar buds off the cedar tree limbs that the loggers cut down. In the winter when food is scarce, cedar buds are the deer's most favorite food. In the summer deer eat clover and alfalfa and other grassy foods. They love to lick salt blocks. The Indians make salt licks for the deer. They hunt and shoot a lot of deer that way. Wiggie and I hunted deer at salt licks once in a while.

I whispered to Wiggie, "It's the rut mating season. I bet that big massive buck will come out pretty soon after the two does." We waited and watched the two does eat about 15 minutes. Then the two does' ears went up and they both were looking back in the woods. Then I spotted a big massive rack of horns standing about 30 feet back in the woods. Maybe seeing the eagles was good medicine. I looked through my scope at the big massive buck, but there was too much brush to get a decent shot at him.

Then the two does started walking to the other side of the road in the cedar cutting and both started eating again. The big massive buck stood there watching the does. He didn't come out in the opening so I could shoot him. All I could see was the tops of the big massive buck's horns. I got butterflies in my stomach again, because I knew the big massive buck was going to go after the two does and soon!

I glanced over at Wiggie and he looked toward the old logging road where the big male black bear went. I looked and another big buck came walking out of the old logging road with his head in the air, sniffing. He must have smelled the two does and the big massive buck, since it was the rut mating season. I didn't think he could smell Wiggie and me, because we were about 10 to 15 feet in the air. He slowly walked toward the two does, but he wasn't as big as the big massive buck. I looked through my scope. He had five perfect points on both sides, a nice big 10-point buck. I thought to myself, *Good. Now the big massive buck will come out in the opening, then I can shoot him*. He would probably fight the big 10-point buck over the two does, but I wasn't going to give him the chance. I would shoot him dead. I couldn't count the big massive buck's points, due to all the brush around him, but as soon as he stepped out in the opening I would shoot him down!

The big 10-point buck walked up to the two does and started sniffing one of the does. Then the big massive buck stepped out into the opening and started walking fast with his big massive rack of horns low to the ground toward the big 10-point buck. I whistled. The big massive buck stopped and looked in our direction broadside. He was about 200 yards away. I put my crosshairs on his big thick neck and shot. The bullet from my bolt-action .300 Weatherby Magnum broke the big massive buck's neck. He fell over dead in his tracks.

The big 10-point buck and both does took off running and jumping toward the cedar woods. I quickly ejected the spent bullet casing and tried a running shot at the big 10-point buck, but I missed him. They disappeared in the thick cedar woods.

Wiggie went jumping down the big rock and ran up to the big massive buck. I reloaded, then put my binoculars and thermos in my backpack, put the backpack on and climbed down the big rock. I slowly walked up to the big massive buck. Wiggie was sniffing him. I noticed he was dark in color. I said, "Wiggie, this is a huge, massive swamp buck." I counted eight long points on both sides, a huge 16-point massive swamp buck.

He must have been in this big area around Vince Shute's property and down by Lost River for at least eight years. Every year white-tailed deer grow a point on their rack of horns. That's how you can tell their age. I was told this by an old Indian, my cousin, Melvin "Rip" King. Back in the 1950's, my cousin Ernie Landgren shot a huge, massive 32-point swamp buck. I counted the points myself when I was 10 years old. He had it mounted and it was hanging on his wall at his home in Nett Lake.

Ever since I saw that huge massive swamp buck's rack of horns on my cousin's wall, I started to hunt deer at the age of 10. That was back in 1966. My oldest brother, Dale Leecy, told me a lot about Vince Shute, but I didn't meet him until I brought him some ducks off Nett Lake in 1968.

I couldn't get over the size of the huge, massive swamp buck's horns. Wiggie started licking the blood from the bullet hole in the swamp buck's neck. I took my knife and started gutting the huge, massive swamp buck out. I grabbed Wiggie and rubbed blood all over his cute little face again. I had to laugh to myself because Wiggie started struggling to get away from me, so I let him go. He rolled around in the grass, trying to get the blood off his face. He got most of it off. I said, "Good hunting, Wiggie." He came over to me and let me pet and rub his cute little head.

I looked at my watch. The time was 3:47 p.m. I said, "Wiggie, after I tie this huge, massive swamp buck off the ground to that cedar tree right there, we have to walk back to the Rabbit Lake Road. Mother will be waiting to pick us up." I pulled the huge, massive swamp buck next to the cedar tree. I took the rest of my nylon rope out of my backpack, tied it around his antlers, and managed to get at least half his huge body off the ground. He must have weighed close to 300 pounds or more with the guts out of him. I'm a pretty strong man. I can lift about 200 pounds over my head. I lifted weights most of my life.

Wiggie and I heard the noisy ravens coming. Sure enough, two of them circled us and landed in the poplar trees not far off. After we left, the ravens would start eating on the gut pile.

When we got to the Rabbit Lake Road, I would have Mother drive down this old logging road and we would pick up both bucks. I thought it might be too muddy for Mother's truck, but decided we could make it. I thought I might even have to borrow Vince Shute's Honda three-wheeler to drag the deer out, but it wasn't that muddy.

When Wiggie and I got up to the noisy ravens, Wiggie and I walked 200 yards across the opening until we could see the big 11-point buck's rack of horns hanging from the oak tree. Wiggie and I couldn't see the gut pile or the noisy ravens, but we could hear them though. I said, "Close enough, Wiggie. The noisy ravens are eating on the gut pile. Let's head back to the Rabbit Lake Road." Wiggie took off back toward the old logging road, sniffing the ground in every direction.

It was three-quarters of a mile back to the Rabbit Lake Road. We went a little over a quarter-mile and Wiggie stopped up ahead with his ears sticking up in the air. He was looking back in the woods. I knew Wiggie saw or knew there were deer back in the woods, so I took my backpack off and tiptoed up to Wiggie. There were five does standing across a clearing on the edge of the woods 150 yards away, watching Wiggie and me. I looked around for a buck but there weren't any standing with the five does or around the area. But I knew there was a buck or two in the area someplace not far off. Wiggie and I watched them for a few minutes, and then they all took off, running and jumping with their white tails waving good-bye, and disappeared in the thick woods. I walked back and put my backpack on, and said, "Good hunting, Wiggie." He started wagging his little tail. I reached down and petted his cute little head, and said, "Lead the way, Wiggie, back to the Rabbit Lake

Road." He took off, sniffing the ground in every direction. We did not see any more deer on our way back.

Around a corner on a straight stretch, I spotted Mother's truck sitting in the road facing our way. I looked at my watch. The time was 5:07 p.m. Wiggie went running up to Mother's truck. She got out and saw some dried deer blood on Wiggie's cute little face. Mother started rubbing the dried blood off Wiggie's face and talking to him. I hollered, "Mother, I shot two big bucks, a big 11-point buck and a big, massive 16-point swamp buck."

Mother all excited said, "Really!" Then she said, "I know you shot a deer because I wiped it off little Wiggie's cute face."

I told her, "If it wasn't for Wiggie I probably wouldn't have shot any bucks! You can drive down this old logging road and we can pick up both bucks. The loggers' trucks make it. It isn't that muddy."

Mother said, "Let's go pick up the deer, then. We have about 1½ hours before it gets dark out. "

I said, "Let's go, then." I took my backpack off and put it in back of Mother's truck. I told Wiggie to jump in the front with Mother and me. I told her, "The first 11-point buck is about three-quarters of a mile back on the right side of the old logging road, about 300 yards across an opening by the edge of a clump of birch trees on a little hill. I will tell you when to stop. You can drive right up to the big 11-point buck."

So Mother slowly drove down the old logging road. I told Mother, "I will give this big 11-point buck to Vince Shute and we will keep the big, massive swamp buck."

Mother said, "That sounds good to me."

We got about a half-mile down the old logging road on a straight about 300-yard stretch. Mother said, "Jim, there are two deer standing on the side of the road."

When I looked, a big buck took off running and jumping. The doe followed the big buck. They ran about 75 yards on the old logging road, and then they went in the thick woods. I told Mother to stop where they ran in the woods. She stopped. We looked for the deer for a few minutes, and then I told Mother to drive on slowly. I told her, "Around the corner there is another straight stretch. There is an opening on the right side. When we get to the opening, the big 11-point buck is tied off the ground to an oak tree."

We got up to the opening and I told Mother to stop the truck and said, "Wiggie and I will get out and you can drive slowly behind us up to the big 11-point buck." She followed Wiggie and me. We heard noisy ravens fighting over the gut pile. We got to within 100 yards and I saw the big 11-point buck hanging. We walked a little closer, Mother following. I saw about eight or nine noisy ravens eating on the gut pile. Wiggie took off running after the noisy ravens. As Wiggie got 20 feet from them, they all took flight, making all kinds of screaming weird noises.

I told Mother to stop the truck. She said, "There sure are a lot of hungry ravens."

I said, "Noisy ravens." Some noisy ravens circled, and some landed in trees not far off.

I untied the big 11-point buck. Mother helped me drag him to the back of her truck. Mother opened the latch on back of her truck and helped me pull the big 11-point buck by the horns. I hollered, "Come on,

Wiggie." He was over by what was left of the gut pile, sniffing around. I told Wiggie to jump in front with Mother and me. I told Mother, "Let's go pick up the massive 16-point swamp buck."

We slowly drove out to the old logging road and took a right turn. Mother drove another three-quarter of a mile. I said, "Around the corner the cedar cutting starts. It's on both sides of the old logging road. There is a straight about 300-yard stretch. The big rock is on the left side of the old logging road. From the big rock, the cedar cutting starts. It goes about a quarter-mile on both sides of this old logging road. By the big rock this little old logging road keeps on going."

When we got about 200 yards from the big rock, I told Mother to stop the truck. The big, massive 16-point swamp buck was hanging half off the ground in a cedar tree. But I didn't tell Mother; I was waiting for her to see it hanging from the old logging road. When I opened my door to get out, Wiggie started scrambling and almost fell out of the truck. He went running and jumping toward the swamp buck's gut pile. Then I saw six or seven noisy ravens take flight. No wonder why Wiggie almost fell out of the truck. He was after the noisy ravens. The noisy ravens were making all kinds of weird screaming noises. They circled and some landed in the poplar trees not far off.

Mother still didn't see the big, massive swamp buck hanging half off the ground, tied to a cedar tree branch. I wasn't going to tell her until she saw it. I said, "Mother, let me back your truck up to an old dead oak tree." So I did and shut her truck off. I told Mother to follow me. I grabbed my .300 Weatherby Magnum and started walking toward the big, massive swamp buck, about 30 yards away.

Then I heard Mother catch her breath and say, "That sure is a huge swamp buck."

I started laughing and said, "It sure took you long enough time to see it."

When we got up to the massive swamp buck, Mother said, "When we get home, Jim, you and Wiggie stand by the swamp buck. I will take a couple pictures of you."

I said, "That sounds good to me."

Mother and I had a hard time loading the swamp buck in back of her truck, but we managed to do it. I said, "Mother, let's head to Vince Shute's. It will be dark when we get there." I looked at my watch. The time was 6:20 p.m., just getting dark as we got to the Rabbit Lake Road. In 10 more minutes we would be at Vince Shute's trailer house. We did not see any more deer on our way to Vince Shute's.

We got about a quarter-mile away from his trailer house, and a big black bear was standing on the side of the road. We could see him well with the headlights. As we drove past him, Wiggie had a low growl in his little chest. Mother and I started laughing just hard. Then I said, "That looks like the same black bear we saw walk around the big rock Wiggie and I were sitting on. Wiggie started growling the same way. I told Wiggie to stop growling, that is one of Vince Shute's pet black bears."

Vince saw our headlights coming, so he came outside as we pulled up to his trailer house. He shined a flashlight at Mother's truck, and as I got out he said, "Jim Chavers and his good little hunting dog Wiggie and Ms. Chavers, what brings you to visit?"

I said, "I brought you a big 11-point buck and I will keep the big massive 16-point swamp buck."

Vince Shute got excited and shined his flashlight in back of Mother's truck. "My God," he said, "you shot that big swamp buck I've seen a few times down by Lost River up in them big rocky hills."

I told Vince Shute and Mother about our good hunting trip at the big rock. I said, "If it wasn't for Wiggie, I wouldn't have shot both these big bucks."

Vince said, "Ms. Chavers, drive your truck up to my shed right there. "

Vince had three sheds and his trailer house. He shined his flashlight at his shed. Wiggie and I followed Vince over to his shed as Mother drove her truck behind us. Vince opened his shed as I dragged the big 11-point buck out of the back of Mother's truck. Vince came over and we both pulled the big 11-point buck by the horns inside his garage.

Mother and Wiggie came over and we talked with Vince for a few minutes, then Mother said, "We have to get home and take care of this big swamp buck."

So Vince Shute shook my hand and reached down and rubbed little Wiggie's cute head and said, "Thanks for the big buck, and thank you too, Ms. Chavers. "

Mother said, "See you later, Vince."

Wiggie and I both got in the truck and Mother drove home. It was 8:05 p.m. when Mother drove in her yard. Wiggie jumped out and ran around the house to check out his territory. Mother and I went inside the house. She turned the lights on and said, "Jim, there are some hamburgers and French fries in the oven so warm them up." I turned the oven on. Mother said, "I'll take a few pictures of you and Wiggie when the sun comes out."

My brother Duze came walking in the house. He said, "I saw the lights on, so I knew you were home. Then I could see some big, massive horns sticking out of Mother's truck, so I walked over and looked in the back. I saw a huge 16-point swamp buck that was shot through the neck."

I told Duze the whole story. Then Mother said, "I will take a few pictures of Jim and Wiggie with the big swamp buck early in the morning, then I will drive him over to your garage, then you can cut him up for us."

Just then we heard scratching on the door, and little Wiggie came running in the house.

DUCK HUNTING

September 1973, Nett Lake, Minnesota—the world's biggest and best wild rice crop

Back in early September 1973, about one month before duck season opened, for some odd reason, cinnamon and green-winged teal flew in flocks and were circling Plum Island and would fly off to God only knows where.

My best friend, Myron "Dootsie" came to my mother's house in the morning and asked me if I wanted to paddle out to Plum Island and shoot teal.

I said, "I would, but I don't have any shells."

Dootsie said, "Don't worry, my dad bought me twelve boxes of number four shot yesterday and told me to go shoot some ducks." I looked at my watch. It was still early. Dootsie said I could have six boxes of shells and he would use the other six.

My mother Joey heard us talking and said, "Good morning, Dootsie."

He called back to my mother, "Same to you, Joey."

My mother said, "Roast duck and wild rice stuffing sounds really good, don't it, Dootsie?"

Dootsie said, "I can almost taste it already."

I said, "Let's have some hot coffee first, then we will go." My mother and Dootsie looked at each other and smiled just big.

It was a rainy, misty, dark day out, good for hunting ducks. As I was getting ready, Mother and Dootsie went in the kitchen and poured coffee. My mother hollered, "I will make you and Dootsie ham-and-cheese sandwiches."

I hollered back, "Sounds good to me."

I grabbed my Remington 12-gauge pump shotgun. Dootsie and I had the same kind of 12-gauge shotguns. By my watch it was 8:00 a.m. I put my binoculars, thermos of coffee, three sandwiches apiece, in my backpack. Then I asked Mother for a ride to Dootsie's to get his gun and shells, 25 decoys and paddles. Dootsie said his father's canoe was down at Big Point.

Mother gave us a ride. We picked up Dootsie's hunting gear and headed to Big Point Landing. We loaded everything in the canoe. My mother wished us luck on our duck-hunting trip. Then she asked, "What time will you be back?"

I said, "You know me and Dootsie. We've been on many good duck-hunting trips before. You never know what time or at which landing we'll come in."

My mother said, "Jim, you are right about that. Well, walk to the house, and then we will pick up the canoe and drop it off at Dootsie's house."

I said, "Okay, Mother." Then she left.

Dootsie gave me six boxes of shells, and then we loaded our 12-gauge shotguns. Dootsie paddled in the back and I paddled in the front. We had a good wild ricing season that year, but it doesn't start ricing until around September 8th or later. It was September 5, 1973.

Dootsie pointed to a flock of local bluebills flying toward Big Island, which was about three-quarters of a mile away. The northern bluebills coming out of Alaska or Canada start their migration south around October 10th or later. The local bluebills hang around in Minnesota and other states. The northern bluebill has a big white chest, where the local bluebill's chest is dull in color. Big Island is about a half-mile long and a quarter-mile wide. Plum Island is a very small island that grows plums on it. Plum Island is about a 1½-mile paddle from Big Point and about a quarter-mile away from Big Island on the north end.

We were paddling about a quarter-mile out, heading toward Plum Island, getting to the thick wild rice. I told Dootsie, "When we get in the wild rice, stop paddling. I will have a look-see with my binoculars and see how the teal are flying at Plum Island."

They were flying in flocks all right. I handed the binoculars to Dootsie. He looked at Plum Island and said, "I got butterflies in my stomach just watching the teal fly by Plum Island."

I said, "Me too." Then we both started laughing really hard.

Dootsie said, "Look, Jim, a flock of local bluebills coming right at us."

We waited until they got in 12-gauge range and we both let them have it. Dootsie and I both shot at the same time and emptied our guns, which held three shells apiece. Four local bluebills fell in the wild rice. Dootsie started laughing and said, "It's going to be another good day for hunting ducks."

We picked up the four local bluebills from the thick wild rice. They were all young local bluebills. They must have been born last spring.

Of course we would shoot a lot of young ducks today. Plum Island was a mile away. The wild rice thinned out in spots, but it was thick in most spots on Nett Lake.

As we were paddling about a quarter-mile away from Big Island, heading to Plum Island, Dootsie pointed at three bald eagles sitting on a big dead oak tree on Big Island. The mother was the one with the white head and tail. It takes five years for the eagles, male and female, to grow white heads and tales. The two dark eagles were the young eagles. The mother eagle was teaching the young eagles how to catch fish and hunt ducks. Our shooting didn't even spook the eagles into flight. Well, they were about a quarter-mile away anyway; they knew we weren't after them.

Dootsie and I continued to paddle toward Plum Island through the wild rice. We were a little over a quarter-mile away from Plum Island when five teal jumped up in the thick wild rice. I quickly grabbed my gun and shot three times, and two teal folded up and fell in the thick wild rice. Dootsie said, "Good shooting, Jim." I looked at Dootsie and winked my eye. We both laughed. Dootsie paddled me through the wild rice to find the two teals. They were small, young, green-winged teals. Then we headed to Plum Island.

It started sprinkling out. The clouds were low and dark. We watched all kinds of ducks fly by out of 12-gauge range. Dootsie and I heard geese honking. They were behind Big Island; it sounded like they were at Fish Creek. The honking was getting closer. Then we saw them: about 40 snow geese, heading past Ash Point, going toward Nett River, which was about one mile north from Plum Island. As Dootsie and I watched them, they climbed high over Nett River and disappeared in the dark clouds.

We watched as flock after flock of young teals flew by, some circling and heading toward Nett River and back the same way they came, young teal exercising their wings for their long migration to South America or wherever they migrate. All of a sudden a big flock of about 20 teal flew past us from behind. We didn't even get a chance to gun down any of them. We watched them and they flew right past the little opening of water at Plum Island and headed toward Nett River.

Dootsie said, "The teal is the fastest-flying duck."

I said, "Without a doubt they are the fastest-flying duck."

Now we were about 200 yards away from Plum Island. I looked at my watch. It was 9:40 a.m. Dootsie and I were both thinking the same thing: no use throwing decoys out. The teal flew by close, some fast, some slow at times. There were about 15 teal sitting in the open water in front of Plum Island. But as we about got in 12-gauge range, they jumped up and flew toward Nett River.

I pulled the canoe into the tall weeds so the flying ducks would not see it. Dootsie slowly walked around to the other side of Plum Island. The wild rice grew thick along the shore all the way to Nett River. There were always a few mallards feeding in the wild rice along the shore.

About five minutes later I heard quacking, then two shots. In the meantime a flock of teal flew right past the open water and headed toward Big Island. That was the second time a flock of teal flew by and I didn't get a shot. Dootsie came around the other side of Plum Island and said, "I shot a green-headed mallard but the other one got away." Then he said, "How come you didn't gun down some teal?"

I said, "I was watching toward Nett River and they snuck right past me."

Dootsie started laughing and said, "That's the second flock of teal that got away without being shot at." Then all of a sudden Dootsie said, "Get down, Jim. Here comes a big flock of teal now."

I said, "Flock-shoot them, Dootsie."

He said, "That's what I'm going to do."

Dootsie and I both shot three times; we emptied our shotguns. Five teal fell in the open water. Three teal were crippled. I told Dootsie to finish off the three crippled teal that were swimming away. Dootsie shot all three crippled teal. Dootsie said I could shoot the next crippled teal.

We were watching the ducks fly into Nett River, coming from behind Big Island and flying through the narrows past Ash Point. The narrows are like three grass islands going behind Big Island, then to Fish Creek. Most of the ducks were young, born last spring. I said, "Flock-shooting ducks is a lot of fun." When there are more than 10 ducks flying in a close group, aim at the front ducks, then shoot. The fine-shot "pellets" spread out and they hit the ducks.

I said, "Dootsie, here comes four pintails flying just above the wild rice from Big Island."

Dootsie said, "I see them."

They turned our way and set their wings to land in the open water. Dootsie said, "Now." We both emptied our shotguns and three pintails fell in the open water, one crippled, so I shot him and put him out of his misery.

It started to rain lightly. Dootsie and I did not have our rain jackets. We got wet but it wasn't cold out, so we were okay.

I took out my binoculars and looked all over Nett Lake to see where the mallards were flying. I first looked through my binoculars behind Big Island through the narrows at Fish Creek. No mallards, just different kinds of ducks. Same thing at Ash Point, and also Nett River. I looked at Wood Duck River for a couple minutes. There were a lot of mallards coming out of the dark, low clouds, diving down into Wood Duck River. I gave the binoculars to Dootsie and told him to look at Wood Duck River and look at all the mallards diving down into the mouth of Wood Duck River.

Dootsie looked for a couple minutes and said, "I got butterflies in my stomach just watching flocks of mallards dive down out of the low, dark clouds and land in the wild rice at the mouth of Wood Duck River."

Dootsie and I were both standing there and all of a sudden we heard wings flapping hard. We both looked up and a big male raven tried to get away. Dootsie shot him and he landed not 10 feet away from me on a rock, deader than a doornail. Dootsie looked at me and laughed really hard. I gave Dootsie a disgusted look.

I said, "Why did you shoot that raven?" Dootsie didn't know what to say.

Dootsie then said, "Let's go shoot some mallards, Jim."

I said, "Let's do it."

Wood Duck River is about 1¼ miles away from Plum Island. Dootsie and I paddled to the other side of Plum Island and picked up the mallard in the wild rice, and then we picked up the five teal and three pintail ducks. The five teal were cinnamon teal. We could have shot a lot more teal that day, but Dootsie and I would come hunt teal another day. The mallards were flying really well at Wood Duck River so we paddled in that direction. I looked at my watch. It was 12:10 p.m.

We watched all kinds of ducks fly in every direction on Nett Lake. We were about halfway to Wood Duck River in the wild rice and four redhead ducks came flying right over us. I shot two times and Dootsie shot once. Two redheads folded up and landed in the wild rice with a splash. We picked up the two redhead ducks and continued our paddling through the wild rice to Wood Duck River.

We were about a quarter-mile away from Wood Duck River watching the mallards flying out of the low, dark clouds and dive down and land in the thick wild rice all around the mouth of Wood Duck River. We could hear them quacking and splashing around by the hundreds. Dootsie and I sat in the thick wild rice, eating ham-and-cheese sandwiches, watching all the young mallards. Dootsie said, "There must be thousands of them eating on the wild rice."

I said, "There is a lot of wild rice for the young mallards and other ducks to eat."

I took my binoculars out and looked down toward Lost River. The ducks were flying all over Nett Lake. I looked at Swamp Island, which was about 1½ miles away; a lot of ducks were flying behind Swamp Island. I looked at Poplar Creek a half-mile away. A lot of ducks were flying in

Poplar Creek, and ducks were flying over the trees to Poplar Creek slough hole, about a quarter-mile back in the woods.

I looked at my watch. It was 1:35 p. m. We sat in the wild rice for 15 minutes, eating and watching ducks. Then I said, "Dootsie, let's go slaughter young mallards."

Dootsie starting laughing just hard and said, "Let's do it. "

I said, "Dootsie, do you think all them mallards are coming out of Poplar Creek slough hole?"

Dootsie said, "No, Jim. If they were coming out of Poplar Creek slough hole, they would be flying over the top of them evergreen trees. The mallards and black mallards and other kinds of ducks are coming out of the low, dark clouds. Stop paddling, Jim, and get ready to shoot some young mallards."

I put my paddle in the canoe, grabbed my 12-gauge shotgun and got butterflies in my stomach. From Wood Duck River going out into Nett Lake there was a channel about eight feet across that went about 200 yards out or so; about 100 or more black mallards jumped up, quaking, about 75 feet from Dootsie and me in the thick wild rice. I shot three black mallards and Dootsie shot two black mallards.

Then over 2,000 of every kind of duck took flight. Our gun barrels got hot from shooting mallards. I will name all of the duck family: black and green-headed mallards, redhead ducks, mergansers, pintails, golden eyes, puddle ducks, butterball ducks, green-winged and cinnamon teal, wood ducks, canvasback ducks, whistler ducks, northern and local bluebill ducks, and coots. Dootsie and I shot only the mallards that took flight. What a wonderful sight to witness.

The ducks flew in every direction for a couple of minutes, and then it thinned out. Dootsie and I shot at least five to seven mallards before they flew off, but I knew from past experience that we wouldn't find all the mallards. The mallards were still diving out of the low, dark clouds in twos, fives, and sometimes 10 or more. They flew right over Dootsie and me, and we shot and folded up mallards left and right. There were so many young mallards flying over us. About every 10 to 15 minutes we got to shoot mallards. White hunters would love a mallard shoot like this.

In front of Wood Duck River, which was about 100 yards away from us, there was hard, marshy ground with a lot of tall weeds. It went about 30 feet wide and 50 feet long. I told Dootsie, "Let's pick up what mallards we can find in the thick wild rice. Then we will go sit in those marshy, tall weeds with the hard ground." We found seven black mallards, 12 green-headed mallards and four female mallards.

Dootsie and I were done looking for mallards, although we both knew there were a few more dead mallards out there. Dootsie and I were about to paddle over to the hard, marshy ground when about 12 young mallards came flying back to the spot where we jumped them. The young mallards would do this if they didn't have an older mallard leading the group of young mallards. Dootsie and I both shot three times and emptied our shotguns. Three young mallards fell in the thick wild rice. One flew away crippled and fell in the wild rice about 300 yards away. I looked at my watch. It was 3:40 p.m. About five pintail ducks and four teal came flying from down Wood Duck River. Dootsie and I let the teal fly by, but we shot three pintail out of the air and they landed in Wood

Duck River. We waited for about 10 minutes, watching ducks fly all over Nett Lake. Then Dootsie pointed, "Here comes a flock of mallards diving down out of the low, dark clouds."

We waited until they got in range and both shot three times, emptied our guns, and three mallards fell in the mouth of Wood Duck River in the open water. Dootsie and I laughed. Then another four mallards came flying out of the clouds. We folded up two mallards; the third mallard flew off crippled and kept going.

We were watching ducks in flocks fly out in Nett Lake. I turned around and looked down Wood Duck River, and five mallards were flying low toward us. I didn't tell Dootsie. When they got about 50 feet in front of us, I shot two times. Two mallards folded up. One mallard hit Dootsie in the chest and almost knocked him over. I busted out laughing just hard. Dootsie gave me a funny look and started laughing hard himself. Then Dootsie said, "Playing games, huh, Chavers?"

I couldn't help it; I started laughing hard again for about 30 seconds. Then I caught my breath and said, "Dootsie, you would have laughed too if you would have seen the look on your face when that mallard hit you in the chest." Then I started laughing again, and Dootsie joined me.

I looked at my watch. It was 5:30 p.m. It would start getting dark out at about 6:15 p.m. Dootsie and I had about a little over an hour left to shoot ducks.

All of a sudden it started raining hard. Dootsie and I were soaked within minutes. It rained hard for about 10 minutes, and then it quit raining just like that. Then a big flock of mallards came diving down out of the low, dark clouds and flew right over Dootsie and me. We both emptied our guns and three mallards fell in the thick wild rice, and two cripples coasted toward Poplar Creek. Dootsie said, "Let's pick up the ducks and count them."

I said, "Sure, why not."

Dootsie counted four local bluebills, five cinnamon teal, two green-winged teal, six pintail ducks, two redhead ducks, and 34 mallards. Then Dootsie said, "Let's head to Girls Landing. We had a lot of fun shooting ducks today. We have 52 ducks that we found. I know we shot close to 75 ducks today."

So Dootsie and I paddled straight across the lake for Girls Landing. Dootsie said, "Now your mother can roast a big pot of ducks with wild rice stuffing for us."

FISHING IN CANADA

1973 (When I was 15)

My coach Bill and coach Joe got school funding to fly high school students 500 miles up into Canada on a fishing trip. The reason why ten of us students got to go on this fishing trip was because we were all on the A Honor Roll.

I got on the high school bus at 8 a.m., heading toward the Orr high school. We drove to the dock at Pelican Lake in Orr, Minnesota where our airplane was waiting. We all had our own fishing rods and our own tackle. Coach Bill introduced us to the pilot and we loaded our fishing rods and tackle on the plane. Then we all headed out on our flight, 500 miles into Canada.

Two miles up in the air, we all looked down and could see thousands of little lakes up in Canada. Orr is only 50 miles from the Canadian border.

We had to stop at the Canadian border customs in order to get into Canada. It took one hour at customs. The air flight border control checked our entire luggage and cleared us to continue our flight into Canada. As we climbed two miles up, the lakes down below were beautiful. We were all bragging about who was going to catch the biggest and most fish.

In 9th grade, Coach Joe was my coach for B squad basketball and football.

In 10th grade I was on the A squad with Coach Bill as my coach for basketball and football. We all played basketball and football for Coach Bill.

It took 1 ½ hours to fly the 500 miles to Canada. It was a five-day fishing trip. We landed on a little lake and unloaded our gear and tackle. We each thanked the pilot and shook his hand. The pilot said he would be back in five days to pick us up.

Coach Bill arranged three big canoes for us on this fishing trip. The boats were waiting for us when we arrived. We helped put three tents up. There were four people to each tent. There was a little boat motor for each canoe. It took us an hour to put the tents up. About 4:00 p.m. we all started fishing.

For an hour, no one had a bite.

I said, "Coach Bill, are you sure there is fish in this lake? I could have fished in Nett Lake and caught 10 pickerels by now!" Everybody laughed. We fished for 10 more minutes when all of a sudden I got a big jerk on my line. As I was reeling it in, I could see a giant Muskie on my line. I got the giant Muskie between two rocks on shore but it broke my line.

My first cousin T-John was in the 12th grade. He was a bully to all of us. T-John tried to grab the giant Muskie by his eyes. He said, "Jimmy, let me get him!"

I said, "No, he's mine!" I said, "T-John, wait, I'll hook up another line to my rod and I'll re-hook him."

T-John said, "No, I'll grab him by his eyes." In seconds that giant Muskie jerked and got away through the rocks.

I start crying and Coach Bill came up and said, "Jimmy, quit crying, I told you there was big fish in this lake." He started to name a few. "Giant Muskie, Northern, Walleye's, Perch, Blue gill's, Croppies, you name it, I caught them all in this lake. That's why we had three boats waiting."

He joked, "Now do you want to go back to Nett Lake and catch your pickerel?"

I said, "No."

Bill said, "Well quit crying and apologize to T-John." So, I did.

I said, "T-John, I'm sorry, do you forgive me?"

T-John said, "Yes, I do, Cousin Jim." And he gave me a hug and I hugged him back. All the guys were standing around watching what happened.

Soon we all went back to fishing. Coach Bill helped me re-hook my line with a Rappel A. Bully T-John caught about a six-pound Walleye. Tom caught a five-pound Walleye. Randy caught an eight-pound Northern. None of the other guys or I caught anything. Coach Bill and Coach Joe told us, "Anybody who caught a fish has to clean out their own fish."

We all agreed. T-John, Tom and Randy cleaned out their fish. That night we all had fish to eat on our first day. After we ate, we told fish stories then we all went to sleep about 10 p.m.

The next morning at breakfast, Coach Bill and Coach Joe told us what we were going to do for the day. "We're all going fishing in the boats." Coach Bill took me, Gerald, Gordy in one boat. Coach Joe had Tom, Dave and Mark in boat two. Since T-John was the oldest, he was the boss of the third boat. T-John, Kevin, Bill and Randy were in boat three.

We all went our different ways out on the lake. We'd fish four hours then we'd meet back at the island. Coach Bill took me, Gerald and Gordy to the north side of the lake where there was a few beaver dams. Gordy and I got off on the shore and took a crossing to the beaver dam. We were fishing five minutes and Gordy hollered, "Jim, bring the net! I got some thing on my line and it feels heavy!"

I set my rod down and brought the net over. But whatever it was broke Gordy's line and got away. I ran over and got my fishing rod with the Rappel A and I came over to where Jonsey lost his fish. We nicknamed Gordy "Jonsey."

Then I cast out my Rappel A. I did not get a bite on the first two tries. On the third time I cast out, I felt a big jerk on my line. Whatever it was on my line, it was really heavy and fighting hard. This time I hollered, "Jonsey, bring the net!" As I was fighting the big fish, Coach Bill came over to the Beaver dam and he helped me land the giant Northern.

Gerald ran over and was watching while Coach Bill helped me land the giant Northern. As I picked up the giant Northern by his eyes, the fish had Jonsey's daredevil lure in his mouth. I said, "Jonsey, here's your dare devil back." Gerald was nicknamed Terk.

Terk, Coach Bill and I started laughing. Coach Bill weighed the Northern; it was 14 pounds.

When we all start fishing again, pretty soon, Terk hollered, "Bring the net!" This time Jonsey brought over the net.

Terk had an eight pound Walleye. Jonsey and I were still fishing on the Beaver house.

Jonsey said, "Look under the Beaver house. Look at all the Northern down there!" He was right; there were at least five Northern in the clear water. I took my Rappel A and let it down in the water. In no time, Jonsey had caught a six-pound Northern.

Coach Bill hollered, "Bring the net!" He was over on the other side fishing by some rocks. Terk brought him the net. Jonsey and I kept fishing. Coach Bill caught a seven-pound Northern. Coach Bill said, "He's going to catch a bigger fish than me before our fishing trip is over."

Another two hours went by and this time Terk hollered, "Bring the net!" Terk had caught a nine-pound Muskie. Then I caught a six-pound Walleye. We all caught a few more fish. (Nothing to brag about.) It was time for all of us to meet back at the island.

This time Coach Joe told a story about their successful catch. Coach Joe caught a three-pound perch and a seven-pound Northern. He told us Tom caught a six-pound Muskie and a four-pound Northern. Then Coach Joe said Dave caught a seven-pound Northern, six-pound Muskie and a four-pound Bass. And Mark caught a three-pound Perch and a five-pound Northern.

Boat 3 came in. T-John had caught a seven-pound Muskie and a four-pound Bass. Kevin caught about a three-pound Bass and a five-pound Northern. Bill caught a three-pound Blue Gill, and a five-pound Northern. Randy caught a three-pound Bass and a big fish broke his line.

Day 3: As we all left to go out fishing again, we headed out different ways, same as we did on our second day. Coach Bill caught an eight-pound Muskie and a three-pound Blue Gill. I caught a six-pound Northern and two three-pound Bass. Terk did not catch a thing. Jonsey caught a four-pound Northern and a two-pound Perch.

On Boat number 2, Coach Joe caught a three-pound Perch and a two-pound Bass. Mark caught a three or four-pound Walleye. Dave caught a five-pound Walleye, a three-pound Perch and a three-pound sucker. Tom caught an eight-pound Muskie, a six-pound Northern and a two-pound Blue Gill.

On Boat number 3, T-John caught two four-pound Walleyes and about a three-pound Perch. Kevin caught two six-pound Walleyes and a three-pound Bass. Randy caught a nine-pound Muskie. Bill accidently hooked T-John by his shirt. You might know bully T-John got mad and knocked him off the boat into the water. After that Randy helped Bill back in the boat. Then Bill caught a few small Perch.

Day 4: It was slightly raining out; Coach Bill thought that he would beat all of us when he caught a twelve-pound Northern. But I beat him by two pounds, with my fourteen-pound Northern. Then Coach Bill caught a four-pound Sucker and about a three-pound Bass. I caught a five-pound Muskie and a three-pound Blue Gill and a five-pound Trout. Terk caught a six-pound Northern, seven-and-a-half-pound Muskie and a three-pound Trout. Jonsey caught a five-pound Trout, six-pound Walleye and a two-pound Bass.

Coach Joe caught a four-pound Northern, two-and-a-half-pound Bass and a seven-pound Muskie. Dave caught an eight-pound Trout, four-pound Northern, two-pound Bass and a two-pound Perch. Tom caught a three-pound Bass, four-pound Sucker and a five-pound Northern. Mark caught a four-pound Trout.

Boat number 3. T- John caught a five-pound Muskie and a four-pound Northern. Kevin caught a six-pound Muskie, seven-pound Trout, four-pound trout and a three-pound Perch. Bill caught an eight-pound Northern, six-pound Northern and a three-pound Trout. Randy caught a six-pound Walleye, four-pound Walleye and a four-pound Northern.

So, we all went back to the island where we camped and fried fish again. Every night we talked and laughed. We all had lots of fun.

About 9:00 p.m., Coach Bill said we should all get ready for a good night's sleep because the airplane was going to be here early in the morning. The airplane was there at 7:00 a.m. and we loaded our fishing gear then we all got on the plane and took off for the border customs. They checked our stuff again, and we flew to Orr, Minnesota.

FISHING LAKE KABETOGAMA

Spring 1974 with my high school class in Orr, Minnesota

When I was in the 11th grade, my classmates got to go on a fishing trip to Lake Kabetogama. There were 36 students in my class but the school had just ten fishing rods for whoever wanted to fish. Fishing season had just started in the spring.

All 36 students got on the bus at 9 a.m. at the Orr high school. Lake Kabetogama is 30 minutes away heading towards International Falls, Minnesota and the Canadian border. Coach Bill was in charge of this trip.

Coach Bill bought suckers for bait at the Lake Kabetogama store. As we got to Lake Kabetogama, five of us that decided to go fishing: Jonsey, Gerald (Terk), Eugene, Randy and me. We all had bobbers and J-hooks. The four guys and I all grabbed the fishing rods and started fishing.

Jonsey and I went to the mouth of the river, where the water flows into Lake Kabetogama. Gerald, Randy and Eugene were fishing about 100 yards away from us on Lake Kabetogama shore.

I put a sucker on the end of my line about five feet from the bobber and Jonsey did the same; we cast them out into the mouth of the river. Gerald, Randy and Eugene did the same thing along the shore.

We were all watching our bobbers and Randy was the first one to catch a six-pound Walleye.

Then Jonsey caught an eight-pound Northern. Gerald caught a four-pound Bass. Then I caught a six-pound Northern. Then Eugene caught a two or three-pound Perch and about five-pound Walleye. Jonsey caught a six-pound Walleye.

I used to raise Hawks and Crows and different kinds of birds in Nett Lake. I heard baby ravens about 300 yards back in the woods. I watched the mother fly over three or four times with food in her mouth. I could hear the baby Ravens making all kinds of noises, while they were eating.

I told Jonsey I was going to go back in the woods and look for the ravens nest. I told Jonsey to watch my fishing rod and my line. It took me about 15 minutes to locate the ravens nest. Sure enough, the mother raven started dive-bombing me. The baby ravens quit making noise before I found the nest. The nest was pretty big. I could tell there was baby ravens in the nest. The nest is about three quarters of the way up in a huge Pine tree. I did not climb the tree but I planned to come back later in the afternoon and take a couple of the baby ravens.

I was gone about a half hour, and walked back out to the mouth of the river and said, "Jonsey, where's my fishing rod and line?"

Jonsey said, "I don't know Jim, it was there about five minutes ago!" Jonsey and I stood around wondering, what the heck happened to my fishing rod.

The water was clear and we could see about fifteen feet from shore. All of a sudden, something caught my eye. I looked down and I could see my fishing rod going by really slow under the water.

The water was cold, but I jumped in anyway and grabbed my fishing rod. As I jumped up out of the water, I pulled on my rod and started to reel it in. I could not tell if it was a Northern or a Muskie. It was huge though. As I got it close to the shore, I could tell it was a big Muskie. I pulled it onto the shore.

Jonsey said," You sure are lucky, Jim!"

Terk, Randy and Eugene came running over to look at my big Muskie. Coach Bill came down and said, "Chavers, I see you caught the biggest fish! I will go get the scale and see how much he weighs."

As Coach Bill went to go get the weight scale, Eugene told me he caught about a six-pound Northern. Randy told me he caught about a five-pound Walleye and a five-pound Northern.

Gerald said, "I only caught one Bass."

Coach Bill came back with the weight scale, I put the Muskie on the scale and he weighed 12 pounds. Everybody said, "You're lucky, Jim. That's a very big Muskie!"

We continued to fish for another couple hours. I was very excited because I caught the biggest fish. Eugene, Terk, Randy and Jonsey said they were going to catch a bigger fish than me by the end of the day. I just laughed.

We all went back to our fishing spots. Then Gerald caught a seven-pound Walleye. Randy caught a snag and he thought he had a big fish on the line. He tried to pull his line in and his line snapped. I laughed, "HA, HA, where's your giant fish?!"

Jonsey caught about a ten-pound Northern, and he thought he beat me by the way it looked. When Coach Bill weighed it up, it was ten-pounds.

Then I caught a six-pound Walleye. Then Jonsey caught another six-pound Northern.

I hollered at Terk, Randy and Eugene, "You guys should fish up here with us! All the fish come through the mouth of the river before they get to open water."

They came over to where Jonsey and I were. I told them about the raven's nest I found and how I was going to come back later and get two baby ravens.

Soon the whole class came over to see what we caught. They looked at my Muskie and Jonsey's Northern.

Someone said, "Jonsey, Jim caught a bigger fish than you!"

I watched the mother raven fly over with food in her mouth heading again towards her nest. We could hear the baby ravens eating back there. I told the class that I went back there and found the raven's nest.

They asked me, "Did you climb the tree?!"

I said, "No, I'm going to come back later and take a couple ravens." They all knew I raised hawks and all kinds of birds. We had only an hour left of fishing before we headed back to our high school.

Gerald and Eugene both caught a fish at the same time. Gerald caught a four-pound Northern and Eugene caught a five-pound Northern. Then I caught another big fish on my line but he broke my line and got away.

Randy asked me if he could fish next to me. I said, "Have at it Randy!" Then Gerald caught a seven-pound Walleye.

I looked at my watch, only 45 minutes left of fishing before we headed back. Coach Bill said we better clean our own fish. We got the scales off our fish and cleaned them out and washed the fish off and got back on the bus.

That afternoon I went back to Lake Kabetogama and retrieved my two ravens.

Gwiingwa'aage

Wolverine (The one that originates from a shooting star)

By Charles Grolla

How the wolverine was named, my fellow Ojibwe told me. Long ago, four spirits were flying through the heavens. One spirit wanted to fly close to earth, because he wanted to scare all the people who lived on earth. But, that one spirit, he flew to close to earth and crash landed on earth. When this happened, a valley appeared. After a few years that valley filled up with water and then grass and trees started to grow around that new lake. So then one day just one wild animal emerged from the water and he was strong and he was fierce. The Anishinaabe never had seen him before that wild animal. But, everybody knew where he had come from that wild animal. Because he (Wolverine) was just like that spirit that crash-landed long ago and because of this, the Ojibwe named him "Gwiingwa'aage." "Gwiingwa" means shooting star and "aage" means where something originates from. Thus, naming the Wolverine "Gwiingwa'aage" means, "The one that originates from a shooting star."

In Ojibwe

Gaa-izhi-wiinind Gwiingwa'aage, Niij Ojibwe gaa-ikidod. Mewinzha, Gii-pabaamisewah niiwin manidoog ishpi-giizhigong baabige dash bezhig gaa-izhi-naazikang gidakiiminaan ji-gosaad iniw anishinaaben. Gii-paashkigamigaadam ozhitood basadinaag. Baabige dash ani-mooshkinebii imaa basadinaag. Gii-zaagakiiwan iniw mashkosiwan miinawaa sa go gaye mitigoog jiigibiig oshki-zaaga'eganiing. Ingoding bezhig awesii gii-pi-mokii. Gii-mashkawizi, aakwaadizi gaye. Anishinaabe gaawin wiikaa gii-waabamaasiin awesiiyan. Gakina dash awiiya anishinaabeg, ogii-gikenimaawaan gaa-onjibaanid. Mii dash, gaa-izhi-wiinaawaad oshki-awesiiyan gwiingwa'aage.

HUNTING A WOLF PACK

Vince Shute had me kill a timber wolf pack that was killing off white tailed deer in his backyard.

Back in the fall of 1973, I took my automatic 22 magnum Winchester rifle with a scope and headed over to Vince Shute's trailer house to ask him if I could hunt deer on his property.

Vince met me outside and said, "There is a timber wolf pack that is killing off the deer on my property. I already caught one timber wolf in a trap." He'd already taken the timber wolf in to have it mounted.

Vince said, "Chavers, you are more than welcome to hunt or trap on my land; you don't even have to ask. You've brought me a lot of deer meat."

I told him, "That's me—I like to ask permission to hunt."

Vince Shute cut me off and said, "Get rid of that timber wolf pack for me."

I said, "That's a deal!" and shook his hand. He said that he could hear them howling back by the big rock or big beaver dam early that morning. The big rock is about one mile from Vince Shute's trailer house. The big beaver dam is about 1 ½ miles away.

"They must have killed another deer," I told him.

Vince said, "I bet they did."

I left my 4x4 truck at Vince's trailer house and took off walking down the old logging road behind his trailer house. The old logging road leads to the Nett Lake Indian Reservation line. The Reservation line is about 2 ½ miles from Vince Shute's trailer house, through an old logging road.

I walked about one mile and I could see the big rock about 300 yards back in the woods. (I shot over 100 deer from on top of the huge rock over 30 years). I thought, *I'll go sit on top of the huge rock and listen for the pack of timber wolves.* I sat there three hours watching, waiting to hear or see the timber wolves, but I did not hear or see a thing. I stood up to leave for the big beaver dam, but a movement caught my eye. It was a small yearling doe; I don't know how she escaped the timber wolf pack. Very lucky I guess. I let the yearling doe pass by.

I walked towards the big beaver dam. Half way there I came across a lot of blood and deer hair. The howling Vince Shute heard - that pack of timber wolves had killed a deer. The pack of timber wolves did not leave any bones behind; it all depends on how hungry they are. Sometimes they leave the head and horns. The deer that the timber wolf pack killed must have been the yearling's mother, without a doubt. I continued walking towards the big beaver dam. I spotted something black moving along about 200 yards from the beaver dam. I got my 22 magnum ready. I waited five minutes then I saw a huge male black bear walking towards me. The black bear weighed close to 700 pounds or more. I know the big male black bear knew I was there because he smelled me. He walked about 50 feet from me then stopped. He looked at me, sniffing the air for about ten seconds and slowly walked away. I got butterflies in my stomach. The big male black bear could have me for supper. I only had a 22 magnum; that would be like a black-jacket bee stinging a person.

I looked at his huge tracks in the mud and next to the black bear tracks, there were timber wolf tracks. I counted three sets of timber wolf tracks in the mud but I knew from past experience there were at least six more timber wolves to this pack.

When I got to Vince Shute's trailer house it was 7:30 a.m., now it was 12:10 p.m. I start walking back to Vince's trailer house 1 ½ miles away. This was not good. I usually see a deer or two coming or going from Vince's trailer house. The timber wolf pack is killing a lot of deer off.

When I got back to Vince's, I told him, "I will be back early in the morning with a bigger gun."

Vince offered and I accepted a hot cup of coffee. I told Vince about the yearling doe and the blood and deer hair I found.

"It must have been the yearling's mother's blood and deer hair I found."

Vince said, "Without a doubt."

I told Vince about the big male black bear that walked up to me and sniffed the air and slowly walked away.

Vince laughed, and said, "Chavers, he could have had you for supper with that B.B. gun!" We had a good laugh. I thanked Vince for the coffee, shook his hand and got in my 4x4 Chevy truck and went home.

I told my mother what Vince Shute said about the timber wolf pack killing and eating all the deer. "He wants me to kill the timber wolf pack off. I told him I would." I also told her about the black bear incident and the yearling doe.

The next day, I left my mother's at 7:00 a.m. This time I brought my Remington 3006 automatic rifle with a high powered scope. It held five shells. I got to Vince Shute's at 7:30 a.m. by my watch.

Vince said, "Come in Chavers, and let's have some hot coffee." He joked, "I see you left that B.B. gun at home and brought a bigger gun to kill that timber wolf pack off with."

I told Vince, "It's a Remington 3006 automatic rifle with a high powered scope."

Vince said, "Good, that will do it!"

Vince Shute told me that he did not hear any howling last night, but said, "I know the timber wolves are out there somewhere."

"I will bet on that! But where can they be?" I said I'd take the old black bear trail towards Lost River and head up into the hilly, rocky country; maybe I will catch them up there.

As I was leaving, Vince said, "Good luck on your timber wolf hunt, Chavers!"

I said, "Thanks, I will need it!"

Lost River is about 1 ½ miles from Vince Shute's trailer house. The hilly, rocky country starts before you get to Lost River and continues past Lost River for a mile or so then the land levels off. I killed a lot of deer in the hilly, rocky country. I walked about a half-mile then sat down on this big dead log and listened. I did not hear a thing.

After ten minutes, I took off walking again after towards Lost River. About ¼ mile from Lost River, the hilly, rocky country starts. The hilly, rocky country starts by the Nett Lake Indian Reservation line and continues about one mile past Lost River then levels off.

I got to the hilly, rocky country; I took another ten minute break and listened. I did not hear anything again. I was about to leave and watched as an owl hawk swooped down and try to catch a partridge, a "grouse." The partridge must have seen the owl hawk coming and somehow dodged the owl hawk. The partridge flew off and lived to see another day. What an awesome sight, Mother Nature plays out.

I looked at my watch—it was 10:30 a.m. I start walking up the hilly, rocky woods. It was beautiful scenery, with birch, pine, cedar, spruces and poplar trees, and a lot of rocks. I sat down on a big flat rock to watch and listen. I sat there for five minutes listening.

All of a sudden, I spotted three large timber wolves, about 300 yards distance, coming straight at me through the trees and rocks. The leader was a big white "Lobo" timber wolf.

Long ago, an old Indian told me, if you kill the leader of a timber wolf pack, the rest of the pack will leave the area and go hunt miles away. I was about to find out if the old Indians were telling the truth.

The big Lobo stopped about 100 yards away from me and sniffed the air for about five seconds. The other two timber wolves did the same thing as the big white Lobo timber wolf did. Then the big white Lobo grabbed the grey timber wolf in his powerful jaws, on the grey timber wolves muzzle, and made him suck hole. The grey timber wolf laid down on the ground like he was in agony. But he was showing the big white Lobo he knew who was boss. Then the big white Lobo let the grey timber wolf up. The grey wolf waged his tail and licked the big white Lobo's muzzle. What a beautiful sight Mother Nature plays out.

Now the big white Lobo was about to come to his death and he didn't even know it. The big white Lobo slowly walked towards me. He stopped about 50 yards away from me. The other two grey timber wolves stopped, too. The big white Lobo knew something was wrong. He started sniffing the air, and the other two grey timber wolves sniffed the air, too. I knew there were about six other timber wolves close by in the area but I did not see them.

I slowly raised my Remington 3006 automatic rifle and put the cross hairs on the big white Lobo's neck and squeezed the trigger "BANG!"

The big white Lobo died in his tracks. The other two grey timber wolves took off running. I got my cross hairs on the big grey wolf and squeezed the trigger, "BANG!" The gray wolf did a flip in the air and lived for about one minute, then died. The third timber wolf got away.

I knew Vince Shute would be really happy that I killed the leader of the pack and another grey wolf. I walked up to the big white Lobo timber wolf and poked him with the end of my 3006 rifle to make sure he was dead. He did not move; he was dead alright. I did the same thing to the grey wolf; he was dead too. The bullet hit the grey wolf high in the upper back and neck area. The big white Lobo timber wolf weighed about 200 pounds. The grey wolf weighed about 160 pounds. They were really big timber wolves.

I dragged the big white Lobo out to the trail to Lost River, and did the same to the grey wolf. I looked at my watch and it was 1:30 p.m. I started walking back to Vince Shute's trailer house. It took me about 35 minutes.

I told Vince that I gunned down the leader, a big white Lobo timber wolf and a grey wolf. I told him the whole story, with a hot cup of coffee. Vince let me use his 4x4 Yamaha four wheeler to drag the two timber wolves back to his trailer house.

I said, "I hope what the old Indians told me is true."

Vince Shute said, "So do I." I gave the two timber wolves to Vince Shute. Then I got in my truck and went home.

Three days later, I went back to Vince Shute's. He said, "The old Indians must have been telling the truth. I haven't heard any wolves howling for the past two nights." Vince shook my hand and said, "Thank you Jim Chavers!"

WOLVERINE STORY

Early December 1974

    I told my mother to keep Wiggie inside tomorrow morning. I felt guilty leaving Wiggie behind when I went hunting deer. But it wouldn't be the first time I left Wiggie home, only to come get him to track down a crippled deer I'd shot. I told Mother I was hunting deer early in the morning at Vince Shute's. I told her my friend Milo saw a big (at least) 16-point buck following two does across the road by the reservation line yesterday morning. They were heading toward Shute's property. The snow was at least a foot deep. That afternoon it started to snow again. Mother and I watched the ten o'clock news that night. It predicted up to six inches of snow that night. By 10:30 p.m., I told Mother, "I better call it a night."

    She said, "Yeah, you better call Wiggie inside so I can feed him in the kitchen. Then you can sneak out the back door early tomorrow morning."

    Mother added, "You know how Wiggie is. He will have a fit if you leave him when he knows you are going hunting."

    I said, "He sure will. He did it many times before." So I called Wiggie inside. I petted his little cute head and his side. Wiggie let Mother pet him too.

    Wiggie usually bedded down in my room at night. I called Wiggie inside my room and shut my bedroom door. I set my alarm clock for

5:00 a.m. Wiggie lay down in his box at the end of my bed. I said prayers and lay down.

I had a dream that night that I would need Wiggie. I couldn't recall the dream exactly, but something told me not to leave Wiggie behind! I woke up to the sound of my alarm clock. I reached over and shut it off. My little Wiggie was sitting by the door as usual, waiting for me to get up to let him go outside to relieve himself and check out his territory. I looked at poor little cute Wiggie for a moment and thought about my dream. *Don't leave Wiggie behind!* I said, "Come here, Wiggie." He jumped up on my bed with me. As I petted him I said, "Do you want to come hunting deer with me at Vince Shute's?"

He started squealing and jumping on my bed.

I put on my pants and let Wiggie out of my bedroom door. He ran straight to the front door. I let him out the door to step into six more inches of fresh snow. I shut the door and could smell fresh coffee and fried deer meat.

Mother said, "Good morning. Sure is a lot of snow."

I said, "Yes, Mother. Good for tracking deer."

I told Mother that I would be taking Wiggie with me. She said, "Oh, in that case, you better feed him."

I said, "Yeah, after he is done checking out his territory, I'll let him back in to eat."

Wiggie was scratching the front door not five minutes later, as I was eating my tasty breakfast. Mother let Wiggie in and fed him by the back door, twice the amount of food she dished out for me. The deer meat tasted good with eggs and pancakes. I looked outside through

Mother's big picture window. It was still snowing out. The fresh snow was very beautiful. God sure created a beautiful world for people to live in.

Wiggie sure ate his food fast. He was scratching at the back door so he could go relieve himself. I finished eating and let Wiggie out the back door, and told him not to go too far away, that we would be leaving soon to hunt deer as soon as I got ready. Wiggie looked at me and got all excited and started jumping around in the fresh snow in the backyard.

I went in my bedroom to get ready, and Mother hollered, "Jim, I put five deer meat sandwiches and a thermos of coffee in your backpack." She brought my backpack in my bedroom and set it on my bed. Then she went back in the living room and continued watching TV.

Since it was snowing out, I dressed warmly, because a few times when I was out hunting or trapping or ice fishing, the temperature dropped from 3 degrees above zero to below zero in a matter of three to four hours. This time I put on my long johns, thermal top, sweater, and snow suit.

I couldn't make my mind up on which gun to use, my automatic .30-06 Remington rifle with a scope, or my bolt-action .270 Winchester Magnum with a scope. They were both good for long range, but the .30-06 was more powerful at long range, so I took my automatic .30-06 rifle. I loaded my gun and put the box of shells in my backpack. I looked at my watch. It was 5:30 a.m., still early. It started to get light out at around 6:15 a.m.

It was time for Wiggie and me to go hunting white-tailed deer on Vince Shute's property. I put my backpack on and Mother wished me good luck on my deer-hunting trip. I kissed her and headed out the back door with my automatic .30-06 rifle in hand. I hollered for Wiggie. He came running from around the corner, all excited, jumping around in the fresh snow. I said, "Let's go find that huge buck Milo saw cross the road following two does yesterday morning."

I took the cover off my GP 433 Yamaha snowmobile. I checked the gas and oil injection. Both were three-quarters full, so I started it up and let it warm up for a few minutes. My sleigh was hooked up to the back of my Yamaha snowmobile. I took my backpack off, put it in the back of my sleigh, also my .30-06 rifle, my power saw, axe, wire and fur traps. I told Wiggie to hop in. He did not hesitate; he jumped in and sat down. I had taught Wiggie to sit down at a young age whenever he rode with me on a hunting trip.

I slowly drove out of the yard in the fresh snow in the ditch next to the main highway. It was three miles to the Nett Lake, Minnesota Indian Reservation line, then about one mile more down the main highway. To the left was a gravel road; that was Vince Shute's road. His trailer house was about 1½ miles down this winding road. People went this way to Vince Shute's. Wiggie and I got to the reservation line and stopped there. There was an old winding logging trail that led to Vince Shute's trailer house 1½ miles away and it was abundant with wildlife.

I could see where three fresh deer tracks crossed the road sometime last night in the snow. They were heading toward Shute's property. One set of tracks was huge. I told Wiggie, "Look at those tracks. I bet that's the three deer Milo told me about." Wiggie got all excited and stood up on the sleigh and sniffed the cold air. I got butterflies in my stomach. I knew it was going to be a good day for hunting deer and trapping fur animals.

There is a big rock about a half-mile away from Shute's trailer house. It was about 100 yards to the right off the old logging trail. The rock was about 10-15 feet in the air. You could see about a quarter-mile in every direction. There were clumps of cedar and birch trees here and there. There were white-tailed deer and black bear trails that went right by this big rock. I had shot a few big bucks and a bull moose from on top of this big rock. Also from the edge of the woods toward the main highway, about a little over a quarter-mile back in the woods, there was a huge beaver dam. I had trapped a lot of fur animals by the big rock and out of this big beaver dam. I trapped fisher, beaver, mink, muskrat, otter, marten, weasel, raccoon, fox, and a few bobcat or lynx.

Wiggie and I slowly rode over our last week's tracks. There were a lot of fresh deer tracks crossing the road in the fresh snow. Off in the distance I could see the big rock. I thought to myself, *Before Wiggie and I go visit Vince Shute, it's the rut mating season for deer. Wiggie and I will go sit on top of the big rock. Maybe I will get a chance to shoot the big buck Milo saw with the two does.*

Wiggie and I pulled up to the big rock, 100 yards from the old logging trail, and I shut off my Yamaha snowmobile. Wiggie jumped out and started sniffing the cold air right away. He had a low growl deep in his little chest. Right away I knew something was wrong. I heard some noisy ravens sitting in the cedar and birch trees. There were maybe 10 of them. About 20 feet off the ground in the birch trees I saw two bald eagles. Every now and then a noisy raven would fly and circle around and land, making all kinds of weird noises.

I figured it was a dead deer's remains, and the bald eagles claimed the dead carcass and wouldn't let the noisy ravens eat. I saw this happen many times before.

I put my backpack on, grabbed my automatic .30-06 rifle, and said, "Come on, Wiggie, we will go sit on the big rock and wait for that big buck Milo saw with the two does. Then if they don't come out, we will go investigate what the noisy ravens are making all the racket about." Wiggie kept looking toward the noisy ravens with a low growl deep in his little chest.

There was a little ladder I made so I could climb up on top of the big rock; I put it on the other side of the big rock. There were fresh deer tracks going in every direction past the big rock. They must have been eating what they could last night. I looked at my watch. The time was 6:25 a.m. Two ravens flew right over Wiggie and me, making all kinds of weird noises. They flew toward the other noisy ravens. I said, "Come on, Wiggie, let's go sit on the big rock and wait for that big buck Milo saw."

We walked behind the big rock. I climbed the ladder to the top. There was a rugged way to the top. I said, "Come on, Wiggie." He was looking toward the noisy ravens.   He came jumping up the rock the same way he did many times before.

It quit snowing. It was a beautiful sight from on top of the big rock. There must have been many white men who felt the same way when they were up in the air in their deer stands. Wiggie and I sat there watching for about half an hour. Wiggie kept staring in the direction of the noisy ravens. All of a sudden we heard the noisy ravens get really loud. The two bald eagles took flight and headed toward Lost River. I said, "Wiggie, looks like that big buck isn't coming out today. Let's go investigate what's dead in the woods back there."

I started climbing down from the rock. About halfway down I slipped, lost hold of my .30-06 rifle, and it fell in the snow. Wiggie came sliding down the same way he ran up. The stock of my .30-06 rifle was sticking out of the fresh snow, so I reached down and picked it up, shook it off, took my gloves off, cleaned the snow out of my scope, and looked through it to make sure the crosshairs were not broken. Then I said, "Lead the way, Wiggie. Let's go see what the noisy ravens are making all that racket about."

Wiggie slowly walked in the direction of the noisy ravens with a low growl deep in his little chest. I had seen Wiggie act like this before when there were black bears in the area. I thought nothing of it because I had one of the most powerful guns in the world in my hands, and an automatic at that! We spotted a fresh set of timber wolf tracks that were taking long leaps to whatever lay dead at the edge of the woods about 200 yards away. Wiggie and I got 100 yards away and about 20 noisy ravens took flight out of the cedar, poplar, and birch trees, making all kinds of weird noises. Some circled; others flew off in the distance.

Wiggie and I got within 50 yards, and Wiggie stopped walking and started growling really loud. All of a sudden, out of a thick patch of cedar trees came a bulky, dark-brown shape with yellowish bands from the shoulders back. I recognized a male wolverine. It came running at Wiggie and me through the fresh snow. I barely had time to point my automatic

.30-06 rifle and fire a shot at the charging wolverine. It did not stop; it kept coming. I tried to fire again but clicked on an empty chamber. Wiggie jumped in front of me and the charging wolverine turned off, leaping and zigzagging through the snow. Wiggie was hot on the wolverine's trail as they disappeared in the thick cedar woods.

I looked at my automatic .30-06 rifle and noticed my clip was missing. No wonder it went *click* on an empty chamber. I bet when I slipped and my gun fell in the snow by the big rock, my clip lay back there in the snow. I took my backpack off, unzipped the part where I kept my bullets, and loaded my rifle, in case the wolverine came back. Then I spotted my little dog Wiggie coming back through the snow. No wonder I had that dream not to leave poor Wiggie at home. Wiggie saved my life!

When Wiggie got up to me, I picked little Wiggie up and said, "Wiggie, you saved my life. I will never leave you home again." I rubbed his little head and ears. I said, "Good hunting, Wiggie. We have to go back to the big rock and find my clip for my rifle. It fell off in the snow someplace."

First Wiggie and I went and looked to see what was dead. Two timber wolves had killed a medium-sized doe and eaten their fill, then headed toward Lost River sometime last night. They left the remains for noisy ravens and other hungry animals. I said, "Come on, Wiggie, let's backtrack to the big rock and try to find my lost clip. Then if we find it, we will go visit my good friend Vince Shute and tell him about the wolverine that got away from us."

Wiggie and I got about halfway to the big rock and already the noisy ravens were fighting over what was left of the doe. We got to the big rock and I started digging around in the fresh snow for my clip. Here Wiggie put his head in the snow and came up with my clip in his mouth. I said, "Thank you, Wiggie," and petted his little head and sides. I shook my clip off, got all the ice and snow out of it, and put it back in my automatic .30-06 rifle. I said, "Wiggie, you saved my life from the wolverine, and you found my clip. You are the best hunting dog I've ever had!"

Wiggie was whining and jumping around in the fresh snow. I said, "I wonder if Vince Shute knows the wolverine is on his property? People have seen wolverines in this neck of the woods, but not too often." This was the first time I'd seen a wolverine. The wolverine is ferocious. It is capable of driving bears or cougars or any animal away from its kill.

I said, "Wiggie, we are very lucky the wolverine didn't attack us. Let's go visit Vince." Wiggie and I walked back to my Yamaha snowmobile. I put my .30-06 rifle in the back of my sleigh, took off my backpack, put it next to the rifle, and said, "Get in, Wiggie." He jumped in the back and I started up my snowmobile and drove to Vince Shute's trailer house.

Vince heard my snowmobile drive into his yard. He opened his screen door and said, "Chavers and his little good hunting dog Wiggie. Come in the house for a cup of hot coffee and cinnamon rolls." He even gave Wiggie a cinnamon roll.

Over coffee, I told Vince Shute about the wolverine. He said, "A couple days ago, just getting dark, a wolverine tried to break into my shed. I chased it away with an axe, since I was chopping wood. A couple years ago I saw a wolverine down by Lost River. He ran across the ice when I was trapping rabbits."

I said, "Vince, I planned on hunting the big buck Milo saw cross the road yesterday morning following two does. I also planned on setting some traps at the big beaver dam."

Vince Shute said, "Now you are talking, Chavers. Maybe you will catch that wolverine."

I said, "Good thinking, Vince Shute, but I have nothing for bait."

Vince Shute said, "Hold up a minute." He walked over to his refrigerator, opened it, then opened his freezer, dug in the back, and came back and set down a frozen bag on the table.

I said, "What's that?"

Vince Shute said, "Frozen rabbit. That wolverine will love this!"

I said, "Now you are talking, Vince Shute." We both looked at each other and busted out laughing really hard.

I looked at the clock on Vince Shute's wall. The time was 8:40 a.m. I told Vince Shute to throw the rabbit in the oven for about 10 minutes to warm it up so I could cut it up in two pieces.

Vince said, "That tells me you are going to set two traps for the wolverine."

I told him, "There are two big beaver houses at the big beaver dam."

Vince said, "I forgot about that, Chavers."

I said, "If I don't catch that wolverine, then maybe I will catch a fox or lynx or bobcat, or maybe even a timber wolf. I will even set a few muskrat traps."

Vince Shute said, "If you catch that wolverine, bring him to me."

I nodded, "I will do that, Vince. If I kill the big buck Milo saw, I will bring him here and give you half."

Vince Shute reached over and shook my hand and said, "Well, thank you, Jim Chavers."

I got up and said, "Wiggie, we have some more deer hunting and trapping to do."

Wiggie started whining and jumping around, then went and stood by the door with his tail wagging. Vince Shute said, "Wiggie sure loves hunting."

I laughed, "So do I." I thanked him for the cinnamon rolls and coffee. Then I remembered the rabbit warming up in the oven. I said, "Hey, Vince, we forgot about the rabbit warming up in the oven. "

Vince Shute ran over to his oven, shut it off, and opened it. The rabbit was half cooked and sure smelled good. Vince Shute looked at me and we both laughed really hard.

Vince took the rabbit out of the oven and ran cold water over it to cool it off. He put the rabbit on a cutting meat board and cut the rabbit in half. He put the rabbit in a zip-lock bag and handed me the rabbit, and said, "Don't eat it either, Chavers, since your Chippewa Tribe is named the Rabbit Chokers." Vince Shute busted out laughing really hard.

I looked at Vince Shute and said, "Wiggie, let's get going before I scalp this white man."

Vince Shute said, "I hope you catch that wolverine or kill that big buck Milo saw."

I said, "I hope so too, Vince Shute," and we all went outside. I put the rabbit in my backpack and started up my Yamaha snowmobile. Wiggie jumped in the back. I said, "Either way, I will be back."

As I was driving away, Vince hollered, "Good luck."

As Wiggie and I got by the big rock, two does took off running through the fresh snow. They got to the edge of the cedar woods toward the big beaver dam within a few seconds and disappeared in the thick woods. Wiggie and I got excited watching the two does run toward the thick cedar woods. I got to thinking, *Maybe those are the two does Milo saw with the big buck. But where is the big buck?* Anyway, I followed to where the two does ran in the cedar woods and parked my Yamaha snowmobile there. Wiggie jumped out and went over to sniff the two does' tracks. I grabbed my axe, eight traps, and wire, and put them in my backpack. I put my backpack on, grabbed my .30-06 rifle, and hollered, "Come on, Wiggie, let's go set traps for that wolverine at the big beaver dam." Wiggie came running and jumping in the snow.

I looked at my watch, now it was 11:20 a.m. I said, "Lead the way to the big beaver dam, Wiggie." Wiggie really was smarter than most people. He took off sniffing the snow toward the big beaver dam. Wiggie and I had hunted deer and trapped fur animals at the big beaver dam many times before. There were a lot of fresh deer tracks in the snow. The big beaver dam was a little over a quarter-mile back in the woods toward the main highway. There were well-used deer trails going in every direction in the woods. There were also fox tracks in the fresh snow. Wiggie would not go more than 50 yards away from me. He would stop, wait until I caught up, then he would take off, sniffing the ground in every direction.

We got to the big beaver dam. There were deer tracks and fox tracks going in every direction. The fox tracks went to both beaver dams, and there were three muskrat houses. I looked at Wiggie and he was standing there looking at something as I caught up to him on the ice of the big beaver dam. I knew Wiggie had seen something. I looked way down about 400 yards on the other side of the big beaver dam by the woods. I saw two does standing there on top of a hill, looking in our direction. I thought to myself, *That must be the two does Wiggie and I saw run this way from the big rock.*

All of a sudden a huge buck with a massive rack of horns came walking over the hill. I quickly took off my backpack. Wiggie was staring in that direction. My brother, Duze Chavers, had sighted in my rifle scope for 500 yards. The big buck stopped and started rubbing his antlers on a little tree. The two does were watching the big buck. It would be a long shot, but I had shot many big bucks about the same distance away. *I bet this is the same big buck Milo saw with the two does.* I waited for the big buck to turn broadside for a heart shot. I didn't have long to wait. I put my crosshairs just below his spine and shot. About one second later I heard the bullet go *thud*. The big buck jumped high in the air and ran back on top of the hill, then took a left turn and ran in the direction of the big rock. The two does ran and disappeared in the thick woods.

Wiggie was already running across the big beaver dam after the big buck. I grabbed my shells and knife and slowly ran through the snow, following Wiggie's tracks. I got to where the big buck had been rubbing his antlers on the little tree, where I shot at the big buck. I saw Wiggie's little tracks in the snow where he was running. Then I saw blood in the snow—not much blood, but I knew the big buck would start bleeding more because he was running. The .30-06 rifle also was one of the best and most powerful deer rifles ever made.

I stopped and listened. Off in the distance toward the big rock, I heard Wiggie barking. I knew Wiggie was fighting the big buck from past deer-hunting experiences. I headed in that direction. I followed the big buck's running tracks. Wiggie's little running tracks were on top of the big buck's tracks. The big buck got on a deer trail that went toward the big rock. The big buck started bleeding more and more. I saw in the snow where Wiggie was fighting the big buck. There was blood all over in the snow where the big buck made charging runs at Wiggie. Then the big buck took off running again. He headed for the open area toward the big rock on a deer trail.

I stopped and listened again. All I heard was noisy ravens off in the distance. The open area was about 300 yards away. I followed the blood trail and Wiggie's tracks to the open area. The big buck had started bleeding badly. He had run across the open area and headed toward Lost River. My Yamaha snowmobile was parked about 300 yards away.

Then I saw Wiggie. He was coming out of the woods on the other side of the old logging road that we rode on that goes to Vince Shute's. Wiggie spotted me. He started barking and stopped and waited for me. I knew the big buck was dead from the loss of blood. I walked across the open area on the blood trail toward Wiggie. I crossed the old logging road, and Wiggie was standing about 200 yards away, wagging his tail, waiting for me. As I walked up to Wiggie, I started petting him and said, "Good hunting, Wiggie." I said, "Go get the deer."

Wiggie ran back in the woods on the big buck's blood trail. I followed the blood trail to the edge of the woods. I could hear Wiggie barking about 100 yards back in the woods, so I walked back there. I saw Wiggie, then a massive rack of horns sticking out of the snow. The big buck died from the loss of blood. I counted seven big points on the left side and six big points on the right side, a big 13-point buck. He must have weighed 300 pounds with the guts in him. The .30-06 bullet only dropped a couple inches. The bullet went through the top of the big buck's lungs and went out the other side. The big buck bled to death.

I leaned my .30-06 rifle against a tree and then I gutted the big buck out. I called Wiggie over. He was sniffing a little tree where a buck rubbed the bark off the tree. He came running over, all excited. I grabbed him and rubbed deer blood all over his little head and face. Wiggie liked that. Then he rolled around in the snow trying to get the deer's blood off him. I laughed really hard. I said, "Come on, Wiggie." I strapped my .30-06 rifle on my back.

I started dragging the big buck by the antlers. Deer are easy dragging in the snow. The big buck must have weighed 250 pounds with the guts out of him. Wiggie followed behind the big buck.

I got the big buck to the old logging road. I left him there. Then Wiggie and I walked over to my Yamaha snowmobile. Two noisy ravens flew in circles by the edge of the woods. They smelled the blood. Soon there would be many of them. I started the snowmobile up, then told Wiggie to jump in back of the sleigh and I drove back to the big buck.

Wiggie jumped out and I shut the snowmobile off. I had a hard time loading the big buck in back of my sleigh. I looked at my watch. Now it was 2:18 p.m.

I still had time to drop the big buck off at Vince Shute's and go set traps for the wolverine and other fur animals. I started up my Yamaha snowmobile and said, "Come on, Wiggie, you can ride up here with me." Wiggie jumped up in my lap and I drove slowly to Vince Shute's.

He heard me drive into his yard. I let Wiggie down. He came outside and saw the big buck. He said, "Chavers, I see you got the big buck Milo saw with the two does. Where did you get him at?"

"If it wasn't for Wiggie, I would never have gotten him." Then I told Vince Shute the whole story. I said, "It's three o'clock. You cut the big buck in half. Wiggie and I have about two hours left before it gets dark out. We will go set traps for that wolverine and other fur animals."

Vince said, "Well, pull up to my big shed. I'll cut the big buck up when you are gone."

"Sounds good to me." I started my Yamaha snowmobile and drove it to his shed. Wiggie came running from the other side of Shute's trailer house. He must have thought I was leaving him.

Vince Shute and I grabbed the big buck by the horns and pulled him out of my sleigh, and we laid him in the snow.

I said, "See you about dark time."

Vince Shute said, "Good luck. I hope you catch that wolverine for me."

"I will give it my best shot," I said. "Get in the sleigh, Wiggie. We have some trapping to do." Wiggie jumped in back of the sleigh and we headed for the big beaver dam.

We parked my Yamaha snowmobile in the same place as before. Wiggie and I saw three noisy ravens flying to the edge of the woods to the big buck's gut pile. I took my automatic .30-06 rifle off my back, made sure it was loaded, and said, "Come on, Wiggie, we're trapping at the big beaver dam."

Wiggie and I followed our old tracks to the big beaver dam. As we came to the edge of the woods, just before we got to the ice, a jackrabbit took off running. Wiggie ran after it. I had to laugh because Wiggie was one time bigger than the jackrabbit. It looked crazy to watch Wiggie chase the jackrabbit. They disappeared in the woods. I kept walking up to my backpack. I hollered for Wiggie. I put my backpack on and walked up to a big beaver dam.

A few minutes later I could see Wiggie come running through the snow. He started sniffing around on top of the big beaver dam. He was sniffing some fresh fox tracks. I took my backpack off. "I will set two traps next to each other with rabbit for bait. I hope to catch the wolverine, not the fox. Even a fisher would be worth more than a fox." I took my axe, two beaver traps, some wire, and the half-cooked rabbit out of my backpack. There was a little opening between the two big logs going down into the ice at the bottom of the big beaver dam. The fox tracks went into this little opening and were digging for something. I wired part of the rabbit on both 330 Conibear beaver traps. Then I ran the wire around the big log, so if I caught the wolverine, he wouldn't get away. Then I set the trap, put it in the opening, and sprinkled snow over the trap so you couldn't see it. I did the same thing to the other trap, but put it two feet away from the first trap.

Wiggie was sniffing around on the other side of the big beaver dam 150 yards away. The fox really dug around on this big beaver dam. I set my .30-06 rifle against a log; I took my backpack off and sat on a log on the edge of the big beaver dam. I opened my backpack up, took out five deer meat sandwiches, took my thermos of coffee out, poured a cup of coffee, and gave Wiggie two deer meat sandwiches. I ate the other three deer meat sandwiches with my coffee.

It was getting late, 4:17 p.m. It got dark out at around 5:00 p.m., so I had time to set two more 330 Conibear beaver traps in hopes to try and catch the male wolverine. The male wolverine was big. He looked like he weighed 50 or 60 pounds. I hoped the beaver traps would hold the wolverine long enough for me to shoot him. I took the rest of the rabbit out of my backpack. I wired part of the rabbit to both beaver traps and then I wired both traps down to a log and set the traps, and sprinkled snow over the traps so you couldn't see them. I hollered for Wiggie. He was off in the distance, sniffing a muskrat house. He came running fast.

It was just getting dark when I finished with the last beaver trap, so I put my backpack on, grabbed my .30-06 rifle, and said, "Lead the way back to my Yamaha snowmobile, Wiggie." Wiggie led the way. "We will go back to Vince Shute's to get our half of the big buck and head for home."

When Wiggie and I got to my Yamaha snowmobile, it was already dark out. I took my backpack off and put it in back of my sleigh, also my

.30-06 rifle, and told Wiggie to get in. Wiggie jumped in the back of my sleigh. I started up my Yamaha snowmobile and drove to Vince Shute's trailer house.

Vince heard my snowmobile drive up, so he came outside. I shut it off and Wiggie jumped out. Vince Shute said, "Chavers, pull your whatever it is up to my shed, and I will put your half of the deer in back of your sleigh."

I asked Vince Shute if he wanted to keep the big buck's 13-point rack of horns. He said, "You keep it, Chavers. You shot it." And Vince put it in back of my sleigh.

I told Vince I set four 330 Conibear beaver traps for the wolverine or fur animals. I said, "It's dark. Wiggie and I will be back in the morning, hopefully with the big male wolverine."

Vince Shute said, "I hope so, and thank you for the deer meat, Chavers."

We shook hands and I called Wiggie, then I started my GP 433 Yamaha up and Wiggie jumped in the back of the sleigh, and I drove toward home.

When I pulled up in the yard, Mother was sweeping snow off the porch with her broom. Wiggie jumped out and ran around the house to check his territory out. I grabbed my half of the buck and Mother held the door open for me as I carried it in the house. I told Mother to come outside and look at the big buck's rack of horns in back of the sleigh. She followed me outside. I picked the big buck's head up by the antlers. She said, "My God, is that ever a big buck." She started counting the points. "It has thirteen points."

I said, "Please grab my .30-06 rifle—it's unloaded—and take it in the house and put it in my bedroom." I put the buck's head in the garage and came back and got my backpack. I was going in the house and Wiggie came running, so I let him in the house. I told Mother the story how Wiggie saved me from the wolverine. Mother was petting Wiggie and rubbing his little head and ears and talking to him.

Then I told her the story how Wiggie spotted the two does, then the big buck came walking over the hill at the big beaver dam on Vince Shute's property. I told her the whole story and how I gave Vince Shute half the big buck, then I went and set four 330 Conibear beaver traps for the male wolverine.

Mother said, "I hope you catch and kill that wolverine for Vince Shute."

"Wiggie and I will give it our best shot," I said. "Mother, I smell fried chicken"

She smiled, "There is fried chicken and fried potatoes in the oven. I will warm it up for you and Wiggie."

I said, "Okay, Mother. I will eat and go to bed. I'm tired. I'll be up early so Wiggie and I can check my 330 Conibear beaver traps."

After Wiggie and I ate our supper, I let him outside to use the bathroom. The clock said 8:25 p.m. Mother said, "I will cook you and Wiggie some cheese omelets, toast, and coffee for breakfast, or do you want deer meat, pancakes, and eggs?"

I said, "Deer meat, pancakes, and eggs. Then you can make us deer meat sandwiches and coffee and put it in my backpack."

I let Wiggie back in, said goodnight to Mother, and called Wiggie into my bedroom. I set my alarm clock for 4:30 a.m., and petted and talked to Wiggie for a few minutes, then went to sleep.

I woke up to the sound of my alarm clock going off. I reached over and shut it off. Wiggie was sitting by the door. I said, "Wiggie, are you ready to go fight that wolverine already?" He came running and jumped up on the bed with me. I knew he had to use the bathroom so I put my trunks on and opened my bedroom door. Wiggie ran to the back door.

Mother was putting deer meat into the frying pan. I said good morning to her and let Wiggie outside. She said, "Good morning, Jim," as she put deer meat in the frying pan.

I went in the bathroom, washed up, and went in the kitchen. I sat at the table, poured a cup of hot coffee, and talked with Mother until breakfast was ready. Then Wiggie came to the back door, so I let him in. Mother dished me up a plate of breakfast first and then fed Wiggie on the back porch.

After I finished eating, I went in my bedroom and got ready. Wiggie came into the bedroom and watched me get ready. I asked, "Which gun should I use, Wiggie, my .270 bolt-action Winchester Magnum with the scope or my automatic Ruger .22 Magnum with the scope?" I decided to take my automatic .22 Magnum with the scope. I loaded it with 18 hollow-point shells. I put the box of .22 Magnum shells in my snowmobile jacket.

Mother said, "Jim, I put four deer meat sandwiches and a thermos of coffee in your backpack."

I said, "Thank you, Mother." I put my snowmobile suit on, and Wiggie and I went outside. I dug in the garage for gas and oil for my GP 433 Yamaha snowmobile. I filled up both tanks then put the gas and oil back in the garage.

I went back in the house. Now it was 5:35 a.m. I told Mother Wiggie and I were leaving before it got light out. I hugged and kissed Mother, put my backpack on, and grabbed my Ruger automatic .22 Magnum rifle. She wished me good luck and said, "Tell Vince Shute hello for me."

I said, "Okay, Mother," and out the door I went.

Wiggie was waiting outside. I put my .22 Magnum rifle in back of my sleigh, also my backpack, and told Wiggie to get in. Wiggie jumped in the back of my sleigh. I started my GP 433 Yamaha, let it warm up for a few minutes, and we drove out of our yard on yesterday's snowmobile tracks.

I got to the old logging road, which was three miles from Mother's house. I drove to the edge of the woods and parked in yesterday's tracks that led to the big beaver dam. I looked at my watch. Now it was 5:50 a.m., just starting to get light. Wiggie was already sniffing around at the edge of the woods where we walked yesterday. I put my backpack on, grabbed my .22 Magnum out of the back of my sleigh, and said, "Lead the way, Wiggie, over to the big beaver dam."

Wiggie and I got about three-quarters of the way to the dam, and Wiggie stopped with a low growl deep in his little chest. I knew what that meant. The big male wolverine might be caught in one of the 330 Conibear beaver traps. I took my backpack off, made sure there was a .22

Magnum hollow-point in the chamber, and then said, "Lead the way, Wiggie."

Wiggie took off walking toward the beaver dam with the hair standing up on his little back. Every now and then I could hear Wiggie's little chest let out a low growl. It was pretty light out now. Wiggie and I could see the wolverine in front of the first big beaver dam, about 150 yards away. I looked through my .22 Magnum scope. The wolverine was eating on a fox caught in my trap. I whispered, "Wiggie, he can't hear us yet."

Then all of a sudden, the wolverine charged Wiggie and me. He was making snarling noises and snapping his teeth together. This time I had a full clip, 18 hollow-point bullets. I let the wolverine get to about 50 yards, and I opened up on him with my .22 Magnum rifle. The big male wolverine rolled around in the snow a few times then lay still. Wiggie went running up to the big male wolverine and tore into the wolverine after he was dead. By the time I got up to Wiggie and the wolverine, Wiggie had his little teeth burrowed into the wolverine's thick fur on his neck. I had to make Wiggie let go. Wiggie acted like he killed the wolverine. I had to laugh to myself. Wiggie was walking around the wolverine with his fur sticking up and still growling. I said, "Wiggie, the wolverine is dead and you killed him." Wiggie started jumping around in the snow. I said, "Wiggie, let's go check the damage on the fox and see if he will be worth keeping."

The fox was caught in both traps and torn to pieces, like I expected. I took what was left of the fox out of both traps and threw the fox over to the side for noisy ravens. Wiggie and I then walked to the second big beaver dam and picked up both 330 Conibear beaver traps. Then we walked back to the dead wolverine. I strapped my .22 Magnum rifle to my back, picked up the dead wolverine, and carried the four traps back the way we came. I put the four traps in one side of my backpack and the wolverine in the middle, and the deer meat sandwiches and thermos on the other side. My backpack must have weighed 80 pounds.

I told Wiggie to lead the way back so Wiggie took off toward the Yamaha snowmobile. I put my .22 Magnum rifle in back of my sleigh, took my backpack off, put it in the back of my sleigh, and told Wiggie to jump in the back. He did. Then I started my Yamaha snowmobile and drove to Vince's trailer house.

Vince was outside shoveling snow. Wiggie jumped out and ran to Vince. He reached down and petted and rubbed Wiggie's ears. Vince asked, "Wiggie, did you and Chavers kill that wolverine for me?"

I said, "That wolverine is so big, he barely fit in my backpack."

Vince said, "Well, let's have a look-see."

"Take him out of my backpack, he's yours."

Vince lifted the big male wolverine out of my backpack. I told him the whole story. Then I said, "My mother told me to tell you hello."

He said, "Tell her hello for me too."

I said, "I will."

I told Vince Shute that Wiggie and I will ride my Yamaha snowmobile down that old black bear trail toward Lost River that way, scouting where to set traps for fur animals. Vince Shute said, "Have at it, Chavers. In the meantime I'll put this dead wolverine in my shed."

I called, "Get in, Wiggie." Wiggie jumped in the back and I headed down that old black bear trail.

Wiggie and I got to Lost River. We could see where two timber wolves had been playing in the snow on Lost River. Maybe it was the two timber wolves that killed the doe by the big rock. They had run in the thick woods. My Yamaha snowmobile must have scared them. Wiggie and I took a left turn on Lost River and headed toward Nett Lake that way. About a little over a quarter-mile down Lost River to the right there is a creek that leads to Lost River's duck slough. Wiggie and I stopped on Lost River. The two timber wolves' tracks crossed Lost River from Vince Shute's property that way. They had walked down the creek, I bet, to the duck slough hole. It was about a two-mile walk from where the doe was killed by two timber wolves through the woods.

Anyway, Wiggie and I headed down the creek to the duck slough, about a quarter-mile away. The two timber wolves' tracks went to the duck slough hole. There was one big beaver dam and three muskrat houses. The two timber wolves' tracks went to the beaver dam and all three muskrat houses. Then they went into the woods toward Lost River. That was when my Yamaha snowmobile must have scared them.

I stopped at the beaver dam. Wiggie jumped right out and went and sniffed the two timber wolves' tracks right away. I noticed a fisher's tracks all over the beaver dam with the two timber wolves' tracks. There were also about a week-old lynx tracks all over the beaver house. He also went to the three muskrat houses. I figured sometime next week I would come back to set traps here for fur animals.

I looked at my watch again, now it was 10:45 a.m. I called Wiggie and he came running from one of the muskrat houses. I opened my backpack and took out the four deer meat sandwiches and coffee. I poured a cup of coffee and gave Wiggie two deer meat sandwiches, and I ate the other sandwiches. While we're eating, two noisy ravens flew over Wiggie and me. When I got done drinking my coffee, I said, "Come on, Wiggie, let's call it a day."

I told Wiggie to get in back of my sleigh and we headed for home.

Later I told Mother how Wiggie and I killed the big male wolverine for Vince Shute, and added, "Vince Shute says hello to you, Mother."

Makwa

(Black Bear) (muk-wah)

By Charles Grolla

The bear is a very sacred animal and is probably the biggest clan among the Ojibwe. The Bear clan was known for being warriors and policemen of the village and the bear signifies strength along with healing medicines and a giver of life. Because of these reasons the bear is not hunted and is only killed when it is greatly needed and a ceremony is usually done before the hunt and a ceremony is done after the kill and remaining body parts are buried. On the Red Lake reservation there is no bear season and bears are not bothered and are rarely killed there, only unless they are greatly needed. When a Bear is killed, there is a rule and tradition that a Bear cannot be killed while sleeping and if the Bear is, it needs to be woken up. The many different body parts on the Bear are used for certain ceremonies. In the spring the Ojibwe hold a special ceremony paying respect and appreciation to the Bear by having a feast for them. There are many sacred stories of the Bear and all the different uses and representations of the Bear.

When a Bear is skinned out it kind of looks like a human being. My great grandmother told me once that Anishinaabeg (ah-nish-inaw-bay-g) (Native Americans) came from Bears or evolved from Bears not from monkeys, I was told this while discussing with her what I had learned at school one day.

KILLING TWO BLACK BEARS

1982, I had to kill two male Black Bears in Vince Shute's backyard.

Back in the fall of 1982, I had my mother drive me out to Vince Shute's trailer house. I told her to pick me up at 5:00 p.m. I planned on hunting deer that day but when I got to Vince Shute's trailer house, he told me there were two big male Black Bears who were aggressive and clawing at his trailer house and trying to get in. They were knocking his garbage cans over and destroying his property. Vince Shute asked me to kill both male Black Bears.

I had a 3006 Winchester automatic rifle with a scope. It held six shells. Vince showed me all the stuff they destroyed and their claw mark's reaching up to the roof. We went into Vince's trailer and had a cup of coffee and Vince told me all the other Black Bears were scared of these two big male Black Bears because they were so aggressive.

I told Vince I would kill the two big male Black Bears for him. I told him how bears like water and said, "I will go to the Beaver dam and wait for them there." Vince Shute agreed with me that Black Bears like to swim in the water. Sometimes these male Black Bears travel together and sometimes they don't. They must have been brothers. Vince thought they must be around 800 pounds or so.

After we finished our coffee, I told Vince that I'd go sit on the big rock because there were deer and Black Bear trails that went by. There was an old road behind Vince Shute's trailer house that led to the Nett Lake Indian Reservation line.

On the way there, I saw three white tailed deer, a buck and two doe's. I could have shot them but I did not. If a bear hears a gunshot, he will go in the opposite direction. I had butterflies in my stomach because I wanted to kill the big buck because that's what I was set out to do in the first place.

Once I got to the huge rock, I climbed on top of it and I looked in every direction for about an hour. Just then, two big bucks came out of the woods and walked right by the huge rock. I wanted to shoot them really bad but I did not. I was waiting for the two huge male Black Bears to come walking by so I could shoot them.

A half hour passed and a huge male Black Bear came walking by the huge rock. I shot him through the heart; he ran about 200 yards tearing up everything in his path, then he finally died. I got off the big rock and walked up to the huge male Black Bear and poked him with the end of my 3006 rifle to make sure he was dead.

I climbed back up on top of the huge rock and waited for his brother to come. But I knew he was not going to come. I also knew he was not far away. I knew he could smell his brother's blood and he knew his brother was dead. Now I knew I had to hunt his brother until I killed him, because he would stalk me and try to kill me.

On the way back to Vince's, I saw a ten-point buck and a small doe. I put the bead on his neck, I shot but I must have just nicked him from 300 yards away. I knew my gun was right on, because my brother Duze Chavers sighted it in for me. I walked over to where I shot at the ten-point buck, but there was only deer hair lying around. No blood.

I got back to Vince Shute's and told him, "I shot and killed one of the bears." I asked if I could borrow his 4x4 Yamaha four-wheeler, so I could drag the bear back to his trailer house.

Vince said, "Sure, no problem Jim! And thank you for getting rid of that Black Bear for me." He gave me the keys.

I drove back to where I shot and killed the big Black Bear. I tied the wire chain around the front paws and neck and hooked him up to the back of the carrier on Vince's 4x4 Yamaha four-wheeler. It was a heavy pull but I finally dragged him back to Vince's trailer house.

Vince said to put the big Black Bear in his garage so he could hang him up and skin him out later. Vince helped me gut him out. This bear must have weighed 800 pounds with the guts in him. We used a wench to get him up in the air, on a tri-pod in Vince's garage.

It was getting close to 5:00 p.m. when my mother Josephine came driving up. I showed her the giant bear I shot and killed. Vince showed my mother the destruction the Black Bears caused and their claw marks reaching up to the roof, right above Vince's door.

I told my mother I would come back the next day and try to kill the other Black Bear. I told her, "I could have killed a couple bucks and a few doe. But I did not want to shoot at them because the big Black Bears would have run away."

Vince shook my hand and hugged and kissed my mother on her cheek and said, "Joey, you sure do have a good boy here."

My mother smiled and said, "I know." Then we headed home.

The next morning at 8:00 a.m., my mother drove me back to Vince Shute's trailer house and dropped me off. Vince shook my hand and said, "Hello Jim, come in and have some coffee with me, before you go slay the last Black Bear." Vince offered me breakfast but I declined because I'd already eaten a good healthy breakfast at mother's house. But I said, "I'll take the coffee though." Vince and I sat around and he told me stories about his pet Black Bears.

Finally I said, "O.K., Vince, I will go over by the Beaver dam and see if the other Black Bear crosses over by the dam, then I will shoot him for you."

On the way to the Beaver dam, I watched two Raccoon's play around for about ten minutes then they disappeared into the thick cedar cutting. About 200 yards from the big rock, I saw a huge Doe standing there. I could have shot her but I did not want to scare the other big Black Bear away. She took off running as I got close to her and she disappeared into the thick cedar woods.

I continued walking towards the big Beaver dam. As I got close to the dam, I found old Deer tracks and fresh Bear tracks. I sat down to wait for the big Black male Bear to come walking along. As I sat there, two Otters came swimming from the far side of the Beaver dam. I watched them play around for fifteen minutes, and watched as they swam to the other side of the Beaver dam and disappeared.

I sat another half-an-hour and saw a huge Buck but he turned around and disappeared into the thick woods. I could have shot him with my 3006 Winchester automatic with a scope but I did not want to scare the big Black Bear away. I waited another half-hour and all of a sudden I saw a big Black Bear swimming from one Beaver dam to the next Beaver dam. Then I knew that this was the Black Bear that Vince Shute wanted me to shoot.

I waited for him to swim to the edge of the bank at the other Beaver dam, and then I put my cross hairs on his chest, on his heart and squeezed the trigger. But I must have shot him below the heart because he did a back flip into the water and got up on the bank and made a mad dash for the brush. He took off running and brush was flying in every direction. I shot at him again, but I missed him.

I walked up to where I shot him but I only found a few drops of blood. Every now and then there were a few drops of blood where he ran. I knew I had to kill this big Black Bear because a wounded bear is very dangerous.

He'd run towards the Nett Lake Indian Reservation line. I waited for about a half-hour then I slowly followed the huge Black Bears trail. I knew the huge Black Bear must have smelled me coming because I heard a bunch of brush breaking where he ran again. I knew the Black Bear must have been hurt pretty bad, otherwise he would have kept running.

I knew I had to kill this Black Bear because I did not want him to destroy Vince Shute's property again, or he might even kill Vince Shute.

This huge Black Bear doubled back on me and was heading straight towards Vince Shute's. I walked out to the old road that led to Vince's and ran down that old road really fast for about ½ mile then I stopped and waited. I waited for about half-an-hour on an old cutting.

Then sure enough I saw the Black Bear come out of the woods on the edge of the old cutting. I put my cross hairs on the big Bears heart again and squeezed the trigger, "BANG!" This time the big Bear was slapping and gnawing on trees and biting his legs and I knew he was dying. Finally the big Black Bear died. I slowly walked up to him and poked him with my 3006 Winchester rifle to make sure he was dead.

I walked back to Vince Shute's and told Vince, "I think I slayed the last big Black Bear." I told Vince Shute the whole story about how I crippled him but I ended up killing him when he was on his way to Vince's trailer house. I'd shot this big Black Bear two times.

A cute bear cub climbing a tree. (Chavers Family Photo)

I borrowed his 4x4 Yamaha 4-wheeler, and dragged this bear back to Vince's trailer house.

Vince looked at him and said, "Yes, this is the other big Black Bear. Thank you for killing both Black Bears for me." He shook my hand.

He helped me gut him out and we hung him on the tri-pod. He must have weighed 750 pounds.

About noon, Vince drove me back to my mother's house. My mother offered Vince some coffee and he drank it and we all talked. Then he shook my hand and thanked me and headed for home.

Mooz

(Moose) (Mooz)

By Charles Grolla

The moose is a special animal when it comes to a successful hunt. The moose's bell is of special importance to the moose and the hunter. First of all a moose being successfully killed by the hunter is seen as a gift to the community and treated as such. There is a great deal of work involved in taking care of a moose, the field dressing and at home packaging and freezing. So one can see how this very large animal is usually a community effort. Once the meat is taken care of and all parts including the meat have been divided up and given away, there is a traditional ceremony and feast done. Usually a, pipe carrier, spiritual leader is asked to smoke and talk for the moose and the moose's bell is used in the ceremony. It is decorated with ribbons sometimes but does not have to be. When the feast is over and ceremony done the moose's bell is taken out in the woods and hung in a tree. Also the head and legs of the moose are placed and tied into the crutch of tree or in the branches near the trunk of a tree about shoulder high and tobacco is placed at the truck of the tree near the ground. The ceremony and feast is the way respect and thankfulness is given to the moose for taking care of the people by giving itself. At the kill site, if it is a bull moose, a male, the male genitalia is separated from the body while field dressing and hung in a tree nearby. Tobacco is placed near the location the moose expired and a prayer of thanks is given to the moose. The hunter usually gives most of the meat away but can keep a good portion and this is the way it is when a moose is hunted. The moose is also a clan animal but it is more numerous in the eastern north part of Ojibwe country.

(Charles Grolla photo of Young Moose)

BULL MOOSE STORY

December 1984

It was 25 degrees, warm for this time of the year. It had snowed about 10 inches of fresh snow. We already had a foot of snow on the ground from the last week. My mother, Josephine, and I were drinking coffee in the kitchen at 8:30 a.m. one Saturday morning. My mother and I were looking out her big kitchen window, talking about all the beautiful fresh snow last night. My mother said, "Jim, there is a car pulling into the yard. The snowplow came through at 8:00 a.m. Who is that, Jim?"

I joked, "I don't know. Wait until he gets out of the car and we will both know."

It was my old friend and cousin Melvin "Rip" King. He was also my mother's friend. He knocked on the door. I said, "Come in." He entered, kicking the snow off his boots. Mother and I said good morning. I said, "What brings you out in this nice snowy weather, Rip?"

He said he just came from Little Fork, on the back road out by the reservation Town Line Road. He said, "A big Bull Moose walked right across the road and walked down the Town Line Road. "

Mother said, "Really?" all excited, and asked, "Do you want a hot cup of coffee, Rip?"

He said, "No, thanks, Ms. Chavers. I just stopped to tell your son Jim about the Bull Moose." Then he said, "Your son Jim is a good hunter. Besides, I have to skedaddle; my wife is waiting for me."

I thanked him for the info about the Bull Moose and shook his hand, and Mother and I both said good-bye.

Then Mother said, "Are you going to go hunt him, Jim?"

I answered, "If you make me some deer meat sandwiches and a thermos of hot coffee."

Mother jumped to her feet and said, "I will make it right now," all excited, "while you go get ready."

So I went in my bedroom, got dressed and grabbed my Remington automatic .30-06 rifle with a high-powered scope, a box of shells, and loaded my gun. I put on my snowsuit and took my gun outside, and warmed up my souped-up 1978 Chevy Malibu. I went back inside the house.

Mother said, "I will put your deer meat sandwiches and thermos of coffee in your backpack. It'll be ready in about ten minutes."

I said, "Good. In the meantime I will go to the store and fill my tank with gas." I asked my mother if there was anything she needed from the store.

She said, "Thank you, Jim, but I got everything yesterday in Orr."

I went and filled up my gas tank and came back to the house. Mother put everything in my backpack and wished me good luck on my Bull Moose hunting trip. Then she said, "I will sharpen up the knives. We are running low on deer meat. "

I said, "If I see a deer, I will shoot him. Then we will have deer meat."

I looked at my watch. It was 9:30 a.m. I told Mother, "I better skedaddle, too, otherwise the Bull Moose will be in Canada if I don't get going." She gave me a hug and kiss and out the door I went, carrying my backpack.

I drove slowly, looking in every direction for deer. It was about 25 miles to the other side of our reservation and the Town Line Road, where "Rip" saw the Bull Moose cross the road. I saw three deer cross the road running. They were heading in the direction of Vince Shute's property, right off the Nett Lake reservation line. I had shot a lot of deer and trapped a lot of furs on Vince Shute's property.

I got to 7-Mile Corner and took a right turn. The other part of the reservation was called the housing site, which was three miles down the road. I got to Sucker Trail Road, and a medium-sized doe was standing on the side of the road looking at me. I stopped my Chevy Malibu about 300 yards away from the doe. I slowly got out of my car, grabbed my .30-06 rifle, put the crosshairs on the doe's neck, and squeezed the trigger.

Bang, the medium-sized doe's head snapped back, and she fell over dead in her tracks. I drove up to the dead doe. The bullet put a huge hole through the doe's neck. There was no bone, only bone splinters. I threw the medium-sized doe in my trunk. I would gut her out later. I had a bull moose to hunt. Well, if I didn't kill the Bull Moose, at least Mother had fresh deer meat to eat.

I continued to drive out to the Town Line Road where the Nett Lake Reservation line ended. As I got to the Town Line Road, sure enough there were fresh Bull Moose tracks in the snow. The Bull Moose had walked on the side of the Town Line Road. There was a straight stretch about a quarter-mile long, and then you came to a hill. Over the hill to the left there was a big cedar cutting. It went about a quarter-mile wide and almost a half-mile long. I'd shot a few deer in this fresh cedar cutting. There was about 30 deer I counted two weeks ago when I shot a 12-point buck. There were a lot of fresh deer tracks crossing the road.

I drove my car to the bottom of the hill then parked it. I grabbed my backpack and .30-06 rifle, got out of my car, put my backpack on, and stood there for a few minutes listening. I could see my breath in the cold air. It was starting to get colder, but I was dressed for cold weather. I looked at my watch. It was 10:35 a.m. I started to follow the Bull Moose's tracks over the hill.

I got to the top of the hill, and there were moose and deer tracks in the fresh snow going in every direction. I looked for the Bull Moose. Then I spotted steam from his nostrils going up in the air about 350 yards away. He was lying down. I looked at the moose through my scope to try and get a neck shot at him, but his hindquarters were in the way, and I didn't want to ruin the meat. I could see his huge rack of horns. If I moved to the left about 30 feet, I would get a neck shot at the Bull Moose.

I started walking to the left. I went about 15 feet and I stepped on some dry ice that broke and made a loud snapping noise. I looked back at the Bull Moose. He stood up really fast and ran toward the cedar woods, 200 yards away. I got my crosshairs on his hindquarters but I didn't shoot. I figured I would track him like I did a few other bull moose and then shoot him.

This Bull Moose was young and smart! As I followed his tracks through the cedar woods, I could see his huge tracks in the fresh snow, like he stood around and waited for me to catch up to him. He went into a swamp, then in some birch and poplar trees. This Bull Moose was taking me in a big circle. Good thing I knew this neck of the woods. He did this to me four times, and I did not see him. He crossed over a lot of fresh deer tracks, then he started heading back to the cedar cutting. I sat down on a big stump and ate a deer meat sandwich and had a cup of coffee. I looked at my watch; now it was 1:10 p.m.

I let the Bull Moose have some time. I waited there for 20 minutes and started following his tracks again. He must have been waiting for me, because I followed his tracks for 10 minutes, then I spotted him. He took off running. I didn't get the chance to get my crosshair on him. He headed toward the cedar cutting, about a half-mile away. I followed his tracks. He walked right through the cedar cutting and down the Town Line Road where he walked early in the morning, when "Rip" saw him. He stood on the road not 20 feet from my car. Then he walked back in the woods.

I looked at my watch. It was 3:35 p.m. It was getting late, and I was tired from tracking the Bull Moose most of the day; I decided to call it a day. I'd hunt the Bull Moose early in the morning. I warmed up my souped-up Chevy, a 350 4-bolt main with 1978 Z-28 racing heads with headers and glass-packs. I rapped off the headers and glass-packs to let the Bull Moose know I was coming after him again.

I drove home and Mother and I gutted out the doe, and I told her what happened with the Bull Moose. I told her I would go hunt him the next morning.

I didn't go hunt the Bull Moose all winter, but I knew he was out there.

BULL MOOSE COLLISION

Late September 1985

My best friend Mike and I played basketball together in school. In 1985, he was going to college at Rainey River Community College in International Falls to study to be a federal police officer (which he is now). We were riding around late one night. He was driving my souped-up Chevy Malibu. Mike asked me if I could drive him to college on the back road. I said, "Go ahead, you are driving." I looked at my watch. It was 1:15 a.m.

Mike looked at the gauges and said, "You have a half tank of gas. I will fill it up in the morning."

I said, "Well, let's hit the road."

We were listening to a cassette tape in the car and cruising 60 miles per hour, going by the Town Line Road off the Nett Lake reservation line. All of a sudden a big bull moose charged my car with his big rack of horns down. I hollered, "Mike, look out."

Next thing I knew, the Bull Moose was on top of my face. My neck and face and the top of my head were hurting bad. The Bull Moose was making all kinds of prehistoric animal noises. He was trying to get off my car. Every time the Bull Moose moved, I could feel his big belly moving around on my face, and I was in severe pain.

Finally his leg must have hooked something on my smashed-up roof of my car, and I could feel the Bull Moose's big belly sliding off of my face, which hurt really bad. His big horn went in the ground, and the Bull

Moose's weight flopped him over the wrong way. I heard Mike say, "Are you all right?"

I said, "No, I think my neck is broken. I'm hurting and I can't move."

Then Mike said, "There is blood squirting out of the Bull Moose's nose. I think he's dying."

I said, "Mike, shut that cassette tape off. There is a big house jack in the trunk of my car. Get it and club the Bull Moose over the head; just make sure he is dead."

Mike said okay, shut the car off and got out of the car. I could taste blood and feel it running down my face. I couldn't move. The car roof was bent back from the weight of the Bull Moose. I had all kinds of little cuts on my head and face from the windshield.

Mike came back and said, "Jim, I think the Bull Moose is dead."

I said, "Good. If you don't get me to the Little Fork Hospital, *I'm* going to be dead."

Mike said, "My head is bleeding too." He showed me his head; there was a little cut on his forehead.

I started spitting Bull Moose hair out of my mouth. My steering wheel saved Mike from getting cut worse. The front shocks were jammed down from the weight of the Bull Moose.

Mike drove me slowly 35 miles to the Little Fork Hospital. They X-rayed my neck and found a hairline crack in my neck. They didn't have to do surgery and put a halo on my neck and head. The next day there was a write-up in the Little Fork newspaper: *Bull Moose Charges Car; Passenger and Bull Moose Both Have Broken Necks; Bull Moose Dies and Passenger Lives.*

The collision happened a quarter-mile off the Nett Lake Town Line Road off the reservation. The Bull Moose weighed 1,200 pounds. They sold the meat in two hours. They gave me the head and horns. The Bull Moose had a perfect rack of horns, nine points on each side.

The doctors let me go home after three days. A cousin Melvin "Rip" King stopped at Mother's house and visited me. Rip told me that the Bull Moose remembered the loud pipes on my car, explaining why he thought the Bull Moose attacked my car.

Rip said, "He remembered when you were tracking him in the snow last winter, and he remembered the loud pipes when you revved your motor up before you left."

"So the bull moose remembered my loud car and charged my car?"

"Yes, he did, Chavers, and it's not because it's the rut mating season. He knew you were hunting him, that's why he charged your car."

Well, I guess I learned another lesson the hard way!

14-POINT WHITE-TAILED DEER STORY

Late October 1988

My best friend, Milo, and I went hunting white-tailed deer a week before we went hunting Bull Moose. We both are Chippewa Indians from Nett Lake, Minnesota. I was told by an old cousin, Melvin "Rip" King, that there was a fresh cedar cutting out on Sucker Trail and it was full of white-tailed deer. "Rip" said yesterday in the early morning, he saw a huge 14-point buck standing on the side of the road. By the time he stopped his truck and grabbed his .30-06 automatic rifle, the huge 14-point buck ran zigzagging and disappeared into the thick cedar woods. I told Melvin I would go get Milo and we would go have a look-see. I said, "Thanks for the info, Melvin," and drove off.

I found Milo and told him what Melvin said.

I said, "Milo, let's take a ride out to Sucker Trail and see how many deer you can miss."

He said, "Okay, chum. Let's stop at my house and get my .30-30 rifle." We stopped at Milo's house and he made us two ham-and-cheese sandwiches apiece, and then he grabbed a box of .30-30 shells and his .30-30 rifle.

We stopped at the Nett Lake Store and I bought soda to drink. I also put $20 of premium gas in my souped-up 1982 Chevy Malibu. Then we stopped at my mother Joey Chavers house, where I lived. I grabbed my 12-gauge pump shotgun. I grabbed a box of 25 slugs and 10 double-ought buckshot. I had five double-ought buckshot under my front seat. I took the core out of my 12-gauge shotgun so it could hold seven shells. I loaded it slug, buckshot, slug, buckshot, slug, buckshot, and slug. The first shot would be slug for long range. Then if we saw a deer close, I would eject the slug, and then it would be buckshot for a close shot. Then I put the shells in my backpack and put it in the back of my car.

Milo and I headed out to the Sucker Trail Road. It was my turn to shoot first; Milo missed the last time we were out hunting deer. It was about 25 miles out to the Sucker Trail Road. We got there and I drove slowly about five miles, then we came to the cedar cutting. It was on both sides of the road. I said, "Milo, I got butterflies in my stomach."

He said, "Me too, chum."

Sure enough, "Rip" was telling the truth. There were deer tracks all over the road. I stopped my car. We both got out and looked at the deer tracks in the road. The fresh cedar cutting sure smelled good. Milo said, "Jim," and made a mad dash for his gun. I looked and I could see three deer running and jumping toward the thick cedar woods. By the time Milo got his gun, the deer had disappeared in the thick cedar woods.

Milo said, "They must have been standing there watching us when we stopped."

I said, "You got that right, Milo. We'll have to keep our eyes peeled."

I looked at my watch. The time was 10:18 a.m. I said, "Melvin told me the cedar cutting was about 300 yards back, with clumps of old cedar trees and poplar, birch, evergreen, and oak trees here and there.

He also told me the cedar cutting is on a windy, curvy road. It goes for about a half-mile long on both sides of the Sucker Trail Road."

Milo and I got back in the car. I was driving along about five miles per hour. The cedar cutting was where the land had dips and ravines, and the land got flat with water back in the cedar woods.

We came to a little hill. Milo did not see the huge buck on his side of the road. The buck was standing about 50 yards down a little hill by the water, watching us drive by. I stopped my car and said, "Milo, there is a big buck looking at us from your side of the road." I grabbed my 12-gauge shotgun, ejected the slug and saw buckshot go in the chamber. I backed my car up until I could see his huge rack of antlers and part of his thick neck, then I stopped the car. Milo put his head back so I could get a better shot at the huge buck. I was aiming at an angle. I couldn't get the shotgun on him too good, so I shot and missed him. The huge buck turned around and ran, jumping and zigzagging down the hill.

I jumped out of my car and shot four more times at the huge buck while he was running away. I thought to myself, how could I miss with buckshot? He did not want to turn in the water, so he ran on the edge of the water and disappeared into the thick woods.

Milo started laughing hard and said, "You missed him, chum."

I said, "I had to hit him."

Milo and I walked down to where the huge buck had been standing, and not a drop of blood. We even followed his running and jumping tracks for about 75 yards and still no drops of blood. Milo started laughing really hard again and said, "Well, chum, looks like it's my turn to shoot first, since you missed the big buck standing really close." Milo busted out laughing really hard again, until I gave Milo a mean look.

Then I remembered about a little over a quarter-mile down the road, there was another road to the right the way the huge buck ran. I went running to that road, but I forgot to grab the five buckshot I put under my front car seat. I looked in the chamber of my shotgun and I had only a slug left. So I walked slowly down the gravel road about 300 yards to see if the huge buck's running tracks crossed the road. I said, "Good, he didn't cross the road." Maybe I was in luck—he might still be in the thick woods. I got butterflies in my stomach. I walked back the way I came about 150 yards, then I stopped and listened for a few minutes. I slowly walked in the thick woods the way the huge buck ran. I walked about 100 yards then I stopped and listened. I looked around really good for a few minutes. I was just about to walk on forward when I spotted the huge buck looking right at me from about 50 yards away in a little opening between two big poplar trees. The huge buck was very smart; he knew I was hunting him. We stared at each other for what seemed an eternity, but it was only about 10 seconds. Then I raised my 12-gauge shotgun to shoot the huge buck in the neck. He looked right, then left, and took off running and jumping toward the road where Milo was. Then he turned and came straight at me. Then he turned again and was going to run by me.

I looked for an opening between some trees the way he was running. I saw an opening between two birch trees about 50 feet away from me. I aimed my 12-gauge shotgun and he was taking long leaps. I timed it just right—I shot, then I saw the huge buck's back legs come over and he skidded on the ground between the two birch trees. I hollered to Milo, "I got him!"

Then I walked up to the huge buck. He started kicking and scrambling around on the ground. He got up and ran toward the road the way I came from. I hollered, "Milo, Milo, Milo."

He answered, "What's up, chum? Did you get him?"

I hollered, "I don't have any more shells." I then yelled, "There is five more buckshot under my front seat. Drive the car around and I will meet you on the road."

When I got to the road I saw the huge buck's running tracks down the side of the road. This time there were blood spots on the road. Milo pulled up with my car. He got out and handed me the five buckshot shells, so I loaded my 12-gauge shotgun. In the meantime I told Milo what happened, and we both followed the huge buck's running tracks down to the road crossing, where he took a right and ran about 150 yards down the right side of the road. He started to bleed more.

Milo said, "He must be a smart, tough old buck. You shot him with a 12-gauge shotgun slug. I never saw any deer or black bear or any animal survive that."

I said, "Me either, Milo."

Then the huge buck took a right turn and went out into the water. We could see the weeds parted which way he was swimming. This huge buck sure knew his territory well. There was a big island he swam out to. The water was all around that island and it was deep too. It was about a 125-yard swim out to that island.

I said, "Milo, that huge buck is not getting away from me. I bet that's the huge 14-point buck that got away from my cousin "Rip." I'm going to swim out to that island and shoot him. Watch this, Milo, you will learn something." We had a good laugh.

I told Milo to run back and get my car. "There is rope in the trunk. I will tie my 12-gauge shotgun to my back and swim out to that island." Milo took off running with his .30-30 rifle to get my car.

Milo stopped my car and opened my trunk and handed me the rope. I cut off part of the rope and strapped my 12-gauge shotgun to my back. I looked at my watch. The time was 1:30 p.m. Then I said, "Milo, keep your eyes peeled on that island. You have the .30-30 rifle for a long shot."

Milo said, "Okay, chum."

Then I slowly took a step in the cold water. Man, the water was cold, but I was determined not to let the huge buck get away and die later from the 12-gauge slug wound. Right away when I got waist-deep in the cold water, I took another step and went in over my head. I came up gasping for breath and taking big, deep breaths. Milo busted out laughing really hard and said, "Well, chum, if you don't get him, it's my turn to shoot." Then Milo busted out laughing again.

The water was really cold since I went in over my head, but I swam out to that island through the green weeds and lily pads. I followed right next to where the huge buck swam until my feet touched ground next to the island. I saw between the tall weeds on the shore where the huge buck headed, so I waited patiently for about five minutes, listening and waiting for my 12-gauge shotgun to dry off. I knew it wouldn't discharge because when I was guiding white duck and geese hunters, we had tipped over right next to shore at Lost River. I had let my 12-gauge shotgun dry off for about five minutes, then a flock of northern bluebills had come flying down Lost River. I had shot two northern bluebills out of the air, so I knew it would work now.

I slowly started stalking the huge buck. The island was about 125 yards long and about the same distance wide; it was bigger than it looked from where Milo was. The huge buck had started to bleed again. I followed his tracks to the other side of the island. I knew I was getting close because I could see the tall weeds and water. I got butterflies in my stomach.

I lost the huge buck's tracks, but I knew he was lying down close by. (Deer lie down when they are hurt bad.) Then I jumped him in the tall weeds by the shore. I turned sideways to get a running shot at him, but I lost my balance and almost fell because my clothes were soaking wet. By the time I got my balance, I heard him crashing through the brush the same way we came from. I did not see him, so I slowly walked the way he ran and I found his tracks. He was bleeding a lot more this time. So I slowly followed his tracks and blood trail toward the other side of the island where we'd came from.

I was getting about three-quarters of the way back the way we started from. I saw a huge rack of horns running and jumping again. He ran about 50 feet away from me. I shot two times at him but he kept running and jumping. I waited a few seconds, and then I heard a splash. He had jumped in the water and was getting away again.

I turned around and I remembered this big dead pine tree that was leaning at a 35-degree or so angle up in the air. I had climbed over it when I was tracking the huge buck. I could see the big pine tree leaning about 75 feet away from me where the huge buck splashed in the water. It was too brushy to see the huge buck swimming away. So I ran up to the big pine tree and climbed about 10 feet up. Then I saw the huge buck swimming away. He was about 75 yards away and about 30 yards from shore. I put the bead between his huge rack of antlers and shot. I almost fell out of the pine tree. I looked and the huge buck was still swimming toward shore. I shot again. The buckshot pellets splashed water all around his huge rack of antlers.

My last shot of buckshot I aimed a little above his huge rack of antlers and shot. I saw the buckshot pellets splash all around him. He rolled over in the water and started kicking and splashing water all around. I knew I hit him and he was dying. I hollered to Milo loud, "I killed the huge buck with my last buckshot shell." I thought to myself, *I shot a lot of deer in my life, but it took about three hours to kill this huge buck with 11 shells.*

Now the bad news: I had to swim out in the cold water and get him. I strapped my 12-gauge shotgun to my back and jumped in the cold water quickly, but the water seemed colder, probably because my clothes were wet. I dog-paddled in the deep cold water out to the huge buck. I counted seven big points on both sides of his huge head. Without a doubt this was the same 14-point buck my cousin "Rip" had seen. I grabbed him by the horn and started dog-paddling with the huge buck all the way around the island in the cold, deep water. Once I got going, it was easy pulling the huge buck in the water.

Milo was standing on the shore waiting for me. He said, "You finally killed him, huh chum, after you shot a box of slugs and buckshot at him."

I said, "Eleven shots and I still get to shoot first." I laughed.

Then Milo reached down and grabbed an antler and helped me pull the huge buck to shore.   That was when Milo noticed he was the big buck "Rip" told me about. Milo said, "Well, chum, we will have to stop at Rip's house and show him this huge 14-point buck." Milo took his knife out and started gutting the buck out while I held his back legs.

I told Milo, "If it wasn't for that big dead pine tree leaning at about a 35-degree angle, the big buck would have gotten away." I told Milo the whole story.

Milo said, "It sounded like a war was going on at that island."

After Milo gutted the big buck out, he rinsed his hands off in the water. Then we both ate our ham-and-cheese sandwiches with soda pop to drink. We looked at where the 12-gauge shotgun slug hit him. It hit him right in the ribcage by the heart, bounced off a rib, and went all the way down his side under his hide and came out by his tenderloin. One double-ought buckshot pellet hit him in back of the head and killed him. Milo said, "It took us a little over three hours to kill him."

We both grabbed an antler and dragged him to the back of my car. Milo said, "Chum, let his huge 14-point rack of horns hang out the back of the trunk on your car and we will ride around the village and show him off."

I said, "Better yet, let's tie him on back of my trunk. Then we'll ride around the village showing him off."

Milo said, "Okay, chum." Then we tied him on the back of my trunk and headed for Nett Lake Village.

Melvin "Rip" King lived a mile out of the village. I told Milo, "We'll stop and show my cousin "Rip" first."

We stopped and "Rip" was parching wild rice. He saw the huge 14-point buck tied to the back of my car. He came walking over and said, "I see you killed him. My God, that's a huge buck. That's the same big 14-point buck that got away from me."

I told Melvin the whole story and that it took three hours to get him. Then I said, "I still get to shoot first." All three of us busted out laughing really hard. Then Milo and I drove around Nett Lake Village showing off the huge 14-point buck.

HE WAS NAMED BIG BILL

(Turkey Day) 1988

We already had four inches of snow on the ground when it started to snow again. It snowed for about an hour, and then it changed to a light blizzard. Tomorrow was November 24th, Thanksgiving Day (Turkey Day). Every Turkey Day I went hunting deer and usually managed to kill a deer or two. But this huge 16-point buck named Big Bill always managed to get away from me. For some odd reason Big Bill didn't grow any more points on his rack of antlers. Every year bucks grow an extra point.

My mother, my sister Jewel, and I were drinking coffee that afternoon at my mother's when a blizzard started. I said, "Good. Early tomorrow morning on Turkey Day I will track down 'Big Bill' in the fresh snow and slay him."

My sister and mother both busted out laughing really hard. My sister Jewel said, "Big Bill with the penny loafers will run circles around you. He has run away from you for how many years now?"

I said, "It will be eight years, but tomorrow I will kill him."

They always teased me. They always changed the name from penny loafers to Converse tennis shoes. I asked Jewel, "What tennis shoes is Big Bill going to be wearing tomorrow?"

She said, "Penny loafers." Then Jewel and my mother started laughing.

I said, "Well, I guess that's what he will be dying in, penny loafers."

My mother said, "Well, I better sharpen up the knives, since you claim you are going to kill Big Bill."

As a matter of fact, my mother and sister named the huge buck "Big Bill," then the whole Nett Lake Indian Reservation who saw him called him Big Bill, too. Big Bill was a sly old buck. He always managed to survive all hunters, even the white man deer hunters.

I stayed home that night. Mother, Jewel, and I watched the ten o'clock news that predicted light blizzards every now and then for the northern part of Minnesota. Before I went to bed, I told Mother and Jewel that my friend Milo saw Big Bill cross the road in his headlights two nights ago. Big Bill was running toward Vince Shute's property. I told Mother to let me off at the Nett Lake Indian Reservation line, three miles from our house in the morning. I said good night to Mother and Jewel, went to my bedroom, and set my alarm clock for 5:00 a.m.

I had a nightmare dream that night. I dreamed I was tracking Big Bill in a blizzard down by Lost River in the hilly, rocky ravines country. I shot him two times in the chest with my .30-30 rifle. Big Bill charged me. I ejected the spent shell and was going to shoot him the third time when I woke up to my alarm clock going off. I reached over and shut it off. I lay there for a few minutes, thinking about my dream. I thought to myself, *It was only a dream. Today I will kill Big Bill!*

I got dressed and went in the bathroom, washed up, then went to the kitchen. Mother was cooking pancakes and eggs with cheese and sausages. She was also making wild rice stuffing for the turkey. She said,

"Good morning, son. I made you three egg-and-cheese sandwiches and a thermos of coffee, and I put them in your backpack. Jewel is still sleeping."

I sat down and Mother served me some pancakes and sausage and eggs. While I was eating, I told Mother about my nightmare about Big Bill. Mother started laughing and said, "It was only a dream."

I said, "Yeah, Mother, you are right."

She said, "Jim, look outside. We got about eight inches of snow from the blizzard last night."

I looked and said, "Good, plus the temperature on your thermometer says 31 degrees above zero, but it is still blizzarding out. Maybe my dream about Big Bill will come true. Only thing, I will kill Big Bill with one .30-30 shot."

I finished breakfast and grabbed my backpack off the stand, then went back in my bedroom and got ready. I grabbed my .30-30 rifle with the scope mounted on the left side; I could shoot with open sights or with the scope for long range. I loaded my .30-30 rifle with six shells and put the box of .30-30 shells in a side pocket of my backpack. I looked at my watch. The time was 5:52 a.m.

Mother said, "Let's go then," and grabbed her jacket and truck keys. I already had my jacket on and my .30-30 rifle and backpack. I put my backpack in back of her truck and brought my rifle up front. Then we headed out to the Nett Lake Reservation line.

It started to blizzard a little harder in the three miles to get there.

Mother asked, "What time should I come to get you?"

I said, "Don't worry about it; I will catch a ride home with somebody."

Mother said, "Well, I hope you kill Big Bill," and smiled.

I grabbed my backpack from the truck and put it on as Mother drove off. I started walking through the fresh snow down this curvy old logging road toward Vince Shute's property. It was about a 1½-mile walk to his trailer house. I walked a half-mile and I came across two sets of timber wolf tracks. They were headed in the thick woods toward Lost River. I walked about a quarter-mile further and I could barely see the big rock through the blizzard. I could only see 100 yards in front of me because the blizzard was getting worse. I thought about giving up the hunt for Big Bill, but I couldn't let my mother and sister Jewel tease me all the time.

I walked over to the big rock, and on the other side of the big rock there were two sets of deer tracks in the fresh snow, about three hours old. I had shot a lot of big bucks and a few Bull Moose from on top of this big rock on Vince Shute's property. From this big rock you could see well for a quarter-mile in every direction. Then you came to cedar, birch, poplar, oak and evergreen tree woods. There was a big beaver dam about a half-mile toward the main highway. That was the way the two deer tracks were heading.

I decided to follow the two deer tracks in the fresh snow, since the weather was bad and blizzarding out. Maybe I would at least kill one of those deer. I would hunt Big Bill another day. I looked at my watch. The time was 8:10 a.m. so I started following the two deer tracks in the fresh snow.

The deer were eating as they went along. They were headed toward the big beaver dam. The blizzard was blowing snow in my face, but I kept going. I followed the deer tracks along the edge and around the big beaver dam, and into the woods toward the main highway. The highway was about a half-mile away and the two deer were heading in that direction, so I continued to follow their tracks.

I got about a quarter-mile away from the main highway, and all of a sudden a huge set of fresh deer tracks started following the two sets of deer tracks in the snow. I got butterflies in my stomach. I thought to myself, *This could be Big Bill's tracks following the two does' tracks, since it's still the rut mating season for deer and moose.*

I followed the three tracks about 100 yards from the main roadway. Then they turned and walked down the edge of another road, the old gravel road to the Nett Lake Indian Reservation. They crossed the old gravel road and went in this big, hilly, rocky area, and the main highway was about 300 yards away from this old gravel road. I thought to myself, *I bet they are lying down or standing around in this big hilly rocky area.*

The wind let up a little bit, so I slowly followed their tracks into this area. I followed their tracks up a hill with trees and rocks all around. Then I spotted a doe looking at me from about 75 yards away by a big rock. I looked all over for Big Bill, but he was nowhere to be seen. Then the doe took off running and jumping toward the thick woods, but I didn't see Big Bill or the other doe take off running. So I walked up to where the doe took off running, and Big Bill's tracks ran toward the main highway, and the two does' tracks in the snow ran toward Vince Shute's property.

All of a sudden the blizzard let up. Just like that, it was a nice calm day, no wind at all. I thought to myself, *Good, now I will track down Big Bill with the penny loafers and kill him*. I got butterflies in my stomach as I slowly followed Big Bill's running tracks toward the main highway, about 300 yards away. Big Bill knew I was after him. He'd eluded me for many years. Big Bill ran through the snow on the edge of the woods next to the main highway for about a quarter-mile, and then he ran across the main highway and headed into the thick woods toward the Nett Lake Indian Reservation line road. Big Bill would stop and wait for me off in the distance, watching me. When I got too close for his comfort, he would take off running through the fresh snow again. I could see his huge tracks in the fresh snow where he stood around and waited for me.

I followed Big Bill every place he went. When Big Bill knew he was far enough away from me, he would start walking. I followed Big Bill's tracks on the edge of the road down the Nett Lake Indian Reservation line. I had followed Big Bill enough times. He always took me in about a three-mile circle; then it would start getting close to dark out so I would give up on the chase for Big Bill. But today it was early out—my watch said 9:35 a.m.—and I had all day, until around 5:00 p.m., when it started getting dark, to hunt Big Bill.

There is a big beaver dam on the left side of the road about a half-mile down the reservation line road, to the left down an old logging road, a little less than a quarter-mile, then you come to the big beaver dam. Every fall I shot a lot of ducks out of this big beaver dam. The Indians call them duck slough holes. Well, I followed Big Bill's tracks across this big beaver dam and up into a hilly birch tree area. I knew from past hunting experiences, Big Bill was heading toward 7-Mile Corner, about 2½ miles away. But then again, Big Bill might head toward Vince Shute's property, the way the two does ran.

I stopped and started thinking for a moment. It was the rut mating season and the two does had run toward the big rock on Vince Shute's property, where I first started following their tracks in the fresh snow. I thought, *I bet Big Bill will head in the direction the two does ran.* So I turned around and bee-lined it for the big rock on Vince Shute's property.

On my way back to the big rock it started to blizzard out again. The ten o'clock news last night sure predicted the weather right. As I got about 50 yards from the main highway, I saw a small doe watching me walk toward the main highway. I stopped and looked at the small doe standing 30 yards away for a few seconds, and then she took off running and jumping toward the main highway. She crossed the main highway in about four leaps and disappeared in the thick woods toward Vince Shute's property.

I looked at my watch. Now it was 10:45 a.m. I followed this morning's tracks on the old logging road to the big rock. I climbed up on the big rock, took my backpack off, and looked all over for deer. Then I kicked some of the fresh snow off the rock and sat down where I had many times before while I was hunting deer. I had shot a lot of big bucks and a few Bull Moose and a few timber wolves from on top of this big rock on Vince Shute's property. The light blizzard stopped blowing snow again and stopped snowing altogether. I looked all over again for deer. Then I opened my backpack and took out my three egg-and-cheese sandwiches and my thermos of coffee. As I ate them, they sure tasted good with coffee. I looked at my watch again, now it was 12:08 p.m. I sat there watching in every direction for a half-hour. Then I heard and saw two noisy ravens making all kinds of weird noises as they flew over me. They didn't even see me sitting on top of the big rock. I sat there for about 20 minutes, drinking my coffee and watching in every direction for deer.

Then all of a sudden, from the corner of my eye, I caught movement. I looked and saw two does coming out of the edge of the cedar woods about 300 yards away. I got butterflies in my stomach as I watched them eating and slowly coming my way toward the big rock. I thought, *I bet these are the same two does' tracks in the snow I started following earlier this morning*. I looked down and I could still see their tracks covered a little by the snow. I could also see my tracks well. I watched these two does eating and slowly coming my way for half an hour.

They were about 75 yards away from the big rock when they both threw their heads up and looked back the way they came from. I watched the two does looking back for a few minutes. Then all of a sudden I spotted a huge rack of antlers thrashing on a small cedar tree at the edge of the cedar woods, about 50 feet back. Then he moved and I could see his huge body and rack of antlers.

As he started slowly walking toward the two does and me, I got really excited and I got butterflies in my stomach, because without a doubt, Big Bill was heading in my direction. Now I knew for sure that these two does were with Big Bill when I jumped them and they had run toward Vince Shute's property. Here I thought Big Bill was heading toward 7-Mile Corner. As I predicted, it was the rut mating season and Big Bill cut across country after the two does.

Now if my sister Jewel and my mother could only see this. Big Bill was walking in his penny loafers to his death.

Big Bill stopped and put his huge head in the air and was sniffing the wind. He was about 200 yards away from me. Then he slowly started walking toward the two does and me again. Within a few minutes Big Bill was sniffing the two does again, about 75 yards away from me. I didn't want to take a chance on a neck shot, since Big Bill had gotten away from me for so many years. I would wait for Big Bill to turn sideways for a heart shot.

I didn't have long to wait. Big Bill turned sideways. I put my crosshairs on Big Bill's heart and shot. Big Bill leaped high in the air, and he came running straight toward the big rock. From the corner of my eye I could see the two does running and jumping toward the cedar woods the way they came. I ejected the spent shell and Big Bill turned about 20 yards away from me. I aimed at his huge chest with open sights and shot. Big Bill took a couple more leaps and fell in the snow. I hollered as loud as I could, "I killed Big Bill with the penny loafers."

I put my thermos of coffee bottle in my backpack and put it on my back, then climbed down the big rock and walked up to Big Bill. I poked him with the barrel of my .30-30 rifle to make sure Big Bill was dead. He was dead all right. I looked at Big Bill's chest and sure enough, my first

.30-30 bullet went right through Big Bill's heart. My second shot went through Big Bill's lungs. He would have bled to death from the first heart shot, but I didn't take that chance. I'd shot Big Bill again.

Big Bill was a big, massive buck. He must have weighed over 300 pounds, with eight big points on each side of his head. So I laid my .30-30 rifle next to Big Bill, took my backpack off, and set it next to my rifle. Then I took my knife out of my backpack and started gutting out Big Bill. After I got the guts out of him, I grabbed him by his horns and had a hard time dragging Big Bill in the snow over by the big rock. Big Bill must have weighed around 275 pounds with the guts out of him. I no sooner got Big Bill over by the big rock when two noisy ravens flew over and circled, investigating my kill. They both landed on a poplar tree about 200 yards away, making all kinds of weird noises. Without a doubt they smelled Big Bill's blood. I wasn't too worried because the noisy ravens would start eating on the gut pile first. But if I didn't come back, they would start eating on Big Bill.

I walked back over by the gut pile. I cleaned the blood off my knife in the snow, and then I put it in my backpack. I put my backpack on and grabbed my .30-30 rifle. I decided to call my .30-30 rifle the Big Bill Slayer. I looked at my watch. It was 2:35 p.m. I walked out to the main highway. I planned on taking some of Big Bill's meat to my good friend Vince Shute. I started walking toward home, and I saw my cousin Melvin "Rip" King coming in his 4x4 Chevy truck. I had made a deer drive last fall to Melvin Rip King on the big rock. We had been after Big Bill, but a big 12-point buck had come running out with two does and Melvin had shot him.

Melvin stopped his truck. I put my backpack in back of Melvin's truck. As soon as I got in Melvin's truck, he saw the excitement on my face. I told him, "I shot and killed Big Bill from on top of the big rock."

Melvin said, "I could tell by the look on your face. I knew you did something good." Melvin started to turn his truck around and said, "Let's go get Big Bill."

I said, "Yeah, then when we drive into Mother's yard, Jewel and Mother will see Big Bill's huge rack of antlers sticking out the back of your truck."

On our way back to the big rock, Melvin's 4x4 Chevy truck made it through the foot of fresh snow in four-wheel drive with no problem. I told Melvin the whole story how I tracked down Big Bill and killed him. As Melvin and I got close to the big rock, two noisy ravens flew off Big Bill's gut pile.

Melvin parked his truck on the old logging road. The big rock was about 50 yards away. Melvin spotted Big Bill's huge rack of antlers sticking up next to the big rock. We both got out of the truck, and I brought my Big Bill Slayer .30-30 rifle with me.

As we both walked up to Big Bill, Melvin said, "Man, Big Bill sure is a big old buck," as he grabbed Big Bill by the horns and examined them. I looked in every direction for deer watching us but I didn't see any deer. Melvin said, "Jim, grab one side of his horns and I will grab the other horn, then we will drag Big Bill to the back of my truck."

I put my Big Bill Slayer .30-30 rifle in Melvin's truck. Big Bill's huge rack of antlers stuck out about eight inches in the air when we loaded him in the truck. I looked around for deer really good, then we both got in Melvin's truck and headed home to my mother's house.

We pulled in my mother's yard. Jewel and Mother were looking out the big picture window. I pointed to the back of Melvin's truck. I could see the look on their faces. Jewel and Mother both went to the back door. Melvin and I got out of his truck. Jewel came out first, then Mother. I hollered loud, "I killed Big Bill with the penny loafers."

Jewel and Mother smiled at me just big then started laughing.

My brother, Duze, came walking from his house. He yelled, "I see you finally killed Big Bill."

I said, "With the penny loafers." Everybody started laughing.

I said, "It took me eight years to finally get a close standing shot at him from on top of the big rock on Vince Shute's property. Mother and I saw Big Bill standing in the ditch by 7-Mile Corner a few times, but we didn't have a gun to shoot him. Seems like he knew when people didn't have a gun. He would stand in the ditch and watch you drive by. But when we stopped, Big Bill would take off running in the woods."

Duze said, "Jim, I will cut him up for you if I can have his hide for tanning."

I said, "That sounds like a good deal."

After we all talked for a while, I told them the story how I was tracking Big Bill down in the snow and shot him from on top of the big rock on Vince Shute's property. I told Duze I had to take a hindquarter to Vince Shute. Then I would give Melvin a front shoulder for hauling Big Bill home for me.

Melvin said, "Okay, let's take Big Bill over to Duze's garage and I will come get the front shoulder later. I gotta skedaddle home. My wife is waiting for me."

I said, "Okay, let's do it."

Acknowledgements

I would like to thank the following people for helping me publish my first book: my publisher Blue Hand Books and editor Trace A. DeMeyer, Patty Shannon who typed my stories, Vince Shute for allowing only me to hunt and trap on his property before the Black Bear Sanctuary opened, and my nephew Charles Grolla for his writing in this book and my other nephews Chris Day and Phil Grolla. I thank my mother Josephine Chavers, my children and all my family. I have many close calls, when I almost died. I have been shot eleven different times! I thank God for keeping me alive.

Jim standing in front of the prehistoric short-faced bear at the North American Bear Center in Ely, MN. The bear was donated to the Center by Randy and Sharon Hartell on May 5, 2007. (Family Photo)

Send letters to Jim Chavers Jr., #168031, MN Correctional Facility, 1101 Linden Lane, Faribault, MN 55021.

About Charles Grolla

"Ogimaagiizhig"

Charles Grolla is Ojibwe and an enrolled member of the Bois Forte band of Ojibwe, an Indian Reservation in northern Minnesota. Charles' Indian name is Ogimaagiizhig which translates to "Chief of the sky" and he is of the Adik doodem (Caribou clan or totem). Charles grew up on the Red Lake Indian reservation but also lived in Bois Forte reservation for a few years during his youth.

Red Lake is a few hour's drive west of the Bois Forte reservation. While growing up in Red Lake Charles learned enough of the Ojibwe Language to get by in conversation; Charles learned from an adopted great-grandmother who was for a time the oldest living full blooded Ojibwe on Red Lake. Charles continued his Ojibwe Language studies at the college level. He completed his bachelor's in Criminal Justice and Minor in Ojibwe Language from Bemidji State University in Bemidji Minnesota. Charles is a lifetime hunter and fisherman and did some trapping, along with assisting his family with commercial fishing in his youth and lived a traditional Ojibwe life growing up.

One of his favorite activities in the winter is snaring rabbits; snaring rabbits is not only a traditional Ojibwe activity but an ancient Ojibwe art and method of trapping.

Charles worked for about 17 and half years at the Department of Public Safety in Red Lake, first as a police officer and then as a conservation officer (game warden).

He is now a teacher in his second year and teaches Ojibwe language and culture at the high school level. Charles is also a lifetime moccasin game player and attends as many tournaments as he can throughout Ojibwe country and enjoys volunteering his time to teach moccasin game to youth and as a community education to the public in the Bemidji, Cass Lake, White Earth, and Red Lake areas. He attends many traditional ceremonies; big drum, midewin, and traditional drum ceremonies and has assisted respected spiritual leaders with ceremonies and cultural functions. Charles lives in Bemidji, Minnesota and is a nephew of the author James Chavers.

Our Ojibwe Language by Ogimaagiizhig

Note: The Ojibwe language that I am writing here in this book is using the double vowel system of writing and reading the Ojibwe language. There are other ways to write Ojibwe but I learned to write the Ojibwe language using the double vowel system. There are many resources that can be used to read and write the Ojibwe language and simple search on the internet can be used to find them.

Awesiiyag / Wild Animals
Waawaashkeshii / White tailed deer
Gidagaakoons / Fawn
Mooz / Moose
Mashkode-bizhiki / Buffalo
Wiisagi-ma'iingan / Coyote
Gidagaabizhiw / Bobcat
Waabizheshi / Pine Marten
Zhingos / Weasel
Makwa / Black Bear
Amik / Beaver
Gwiingwa'aage / Wolverine
Waabooz / Snowshoe Hare
Mayagi-waaboozoons / Cotton Tail
Misajidamoo / Gray Squirrel
Akakojiish / Wood Chuck
Waagosh / Red Fox
Shigaag / Skunk

Adik / Caribou
Adikoons / Little Caribou
Omashkooz / Elk
Ma'iingan / Timber Wolf
Bizhiw / Canadian Lynx
Ojiig / Fisher
Zhaangweshi / Mink
Wazhask / Muskrat
Makoons / Black Bear Cub
Nigig / River Otter
Gichi-gaazhig / Mountain Lion
Misaabooz / Jack Rabbit
Ajidamoo / Red Squirrel
Zhagashkaandawe / Flying Squirrel
Misakakojiish / Badger
Esiban / Raccoon
Gaag / Porcupine

Bineshiinhyag/ Birds
Migizi / Bald Eagle
Gookooko'oo / Owl
Miskogiigik / Red Tailed Hawk
Zhashagi / Blue Heron
Zhiishiib/ Duck
Gaagaashib / Black Duck
Nika / Candain Goose
Maang / Common Loon
Mayagi-bine / Pheasant
Bine / Partridge
Diindiisi / Blue Jay
Ozhaawashko-bineshiinh / Blue Bird
Asiginaak / Black Bird

Giniw / Golden Eagle
Gekek / Hawk
Ajijaak / Sand Hill Crane
Mashka'oose / Bittern
Ininishib / Mallard
Waabizii / Swan
Zhede / Pelican
Zhingibiz / Hell Diver
Omiimii / Mounring Dove
Opichi / Robin
Gijigijiganeshii / Chickadee
Ozaaweshiinh / Gold Finch
Miskobineshii / Cardinal

Common Ojibwe Phrases

Boozhoo / Hello
Aaniin / Hi
Aaniin ezhi-ayaayan? / How are you?
Nimino-ayaa / I am good
Aaniindi wenjibaayan? / Where are you from?
Nindoonjibaa omaa / I am from here
Awenen gidoodem? / What clan are you?
Adik nindoodem / I am Caribou clan
Aaniin ezhinkaazoyan? / What is your name?
Jim nindizhinikaaz / My name is Jim
Aaniin ezhiwebak agwajiing? / How is the weather
Mino-giizhigad / It is a nice day
Niwii-kiiyose / I want to go hunting
 Gigawaabamin naagaj / I will see you later

23348180R00115

Made in the USA
Middletown, DE
23 August 2015